The Craft
and Its Symbols

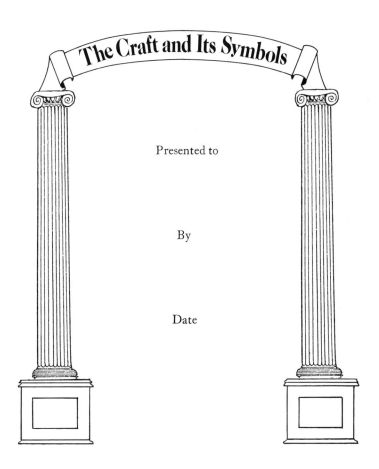

The Craft and Its Symbols

Presented to

By

Date

ECCE SIGNUM *

Men toil along the road of life,
But each one looks with different eyes.
Some note but dross or mud or gloom;
Some see bright Logos in the skies.

A gavel strikes; the trowel spreads
Cement to join the ashlars tight.
Freemasons know they're more than tools;
They point the way to Truth and Light.

Wise Plato taught, the world's unreal;
A thing's eternal in the mind.
Life's candle brief is but a symbol,
By God's immortal love defined.

—CONRAD HAHN

* Behold the Symbol!

The Craft and Its Symbols:
Opening the Door to Masonic Symbolism

Allen E. Roberts

MACOY PUBLISHING AND MASONIC SUPPLY
COMPANY, INC.

Richmond, Virginia

ISBN-0-88053-058-8

Foreword

Symbols are sometimes described as the universal language because they present the message in a way that is understood by all and do not depend on words that are different in various languages. The word "symbol" is defined as a thing that represents something else by association; in Freemasonry it might be defined as a material object that represents a basic moral truth or lesson.

Symbolism is part of everyday living. The printed word is basically a symbol; the driver of an automobile is constantly seeing symbols on road signs; we are constantly encountering mathematical symbols, a blind-folded figure holding scales symbolizing justice, the striped pole indicating a barber shop, etc. Many consumer products are represented by well known symbols. These are so common that we soon forget to recognize the symbols and almost see in our mind's eye the thing sought to be symbolized.

The ritualistic ceremonies of the three Masonic Degrees are the foundation of the world's oldest, largest, and most famous fraternity. In these ceremonies are contained all the philosophy and lessons of Freemasonry, and each stone in the foundation is a symbol of one kind or another. Many of the symbols are called to the attention of the new member as the degrees are being conferred, but there is much to the ceremony that does not meet the eye at the time, so that a study of the subject is intriguing as one finds new gold while conducting the search.

Brother Allen E. Roberts has been a Freemason for many years. With a keen inquiring mind he early sensed the importance of the symbolism of the Craft and started a detailed study of it. We are fortunate that he has reduced these thoughts to a format that can be enjoyed by us all. A great deal that is contained in this book is not new, but since the material is covered in chronological order as the ceremony of Initiation, Passing, and Raising takes place, it enables us to see more than we saw when first exposed to the material.

This fine presentation will make the ceremony of the three degrees understandable and more meaningful. For the new member, it offers an adventure in re-living these experiences and an opportunity to review the lessons taught at the time. For the older member, it presents a golden opportunity for a renewal of old ideas and opening the door for further light on the subject.

Because of the prevalence of "horse-play" in the initiation ceremonies of many college fraternities, sometimes the non-Mason assumes that the initiation ceremonies of Freemasonry are for the amusement of the members. This is not true, because the ceremonies are serious and are designed to teach in a unique and most effective manner basic moral lessons. This book clearly indicates that this is the purpose of the ceremony of the three Masonic degrees.

Everything connected with the ceremonies of Freemasonry have a symbolic meaning. Take for example the act of the candidate removing his shoes before the commencement of the ceremony; it has a symbolic meaning. The act of the candidate walking around the Lodge room also has a symbolic meaning. These two illustrations of parts of the ceremony are not readily recognized at the time of the experience by the candidate. This book calls attention to these two items as well as others and explains their symbolic significance.

An informed Mason is a better Mason. The new member who studies this book will have a better understanding of the ceremonies of the Craft, of the symbolism woven into the entire fabric of Freemasonry, and develop a deeper appreciation of the meaning of the three experiences which brought him to the summit of becoming a Master Mason.

—Alphonse Cerza

Preface

Why this book? Because symbolism is the life-blood of the Craft. It is what distinguishes Freemasonry from other fraternal organizations. It is the principal vehicle by which the ritual teaches Masonic philosophy and moral lessons. Masonic symbolism is unique.

I was *asked* to write this book. A distinction, I might add, in this day when millions of words have been written, or copied, or slightly rephrased, on Freemasonry. The Macoy Publishing and Masonic Supply Company, Inc. felt there was a definite need for a modern approach. A book with illustrations (old and new) which would help the newly raised Master Mason to a better understanding of the meaning and teachings of the ceremonies through which he had recently passed. A book written simply without the profuse occult meanings (which too often only add to his already present confusion). And, yet, a volume to inspire him, make him eager to pursue his Masonic education that he might learn more of the glorious teachings of our Craft for his further enrichment in his daily pursuits.

Earlier authors have delved into the ancient mysteries in great depth. So, what to leave out of this volume has been a problem. My good friend and Masonic teacher, Alphonse Cerza, helped me to decide when he said: "Some books go out into a far-fetched field of imagination and develop explanations and theories that are sometimes ridiculous. They often delve into the occult and see much more than is intended in any simple object."

I agree with Brother Cerza. This book, therefore, is written to help the new Master Mason to understand what Masonic symbolism means. Hopefully, it will be the beginning of his search for more and more light in Freemasonry.

I hope my efforts will be of help to the new members so they will not be as frustrated as I was twenty-five years ago. Too many of my brethren thought I was crazy when I asked how I could find books on Freemasonry. My lodge had no library, and those I talked to didn't know where I could find Masonic books. This seems strange to me now. There are plenty of volumes available and my personal library is fairly extensive. But I find as I travel around the country that what I went through when I was Raised is still a problem.

This book is intended merely to be the beginning of a long journey into the Masonic literature available today.

I have deliberately consulted no other books on Masonic symbolism in writing this. I won't claim they haven't influenced me. I've read many in years gone by. I have relied on publications of The Masonic Service Association and found them extremely valuable. These, along with the wise counsel of Conrad Hahn, Walter M. Callaway, Jr., and Alphonse Cerza, had a large part in shaping this book. Dr. Louis H. Manarin, State Archivist of the Commonwealth of Virginia, who, as I write this, is receiving his degrees, helped proof read the final draft, and page proofs. To all of them I owe more than I can repay.

My daughter, Marcia, spent many hours typing different drafts of the manuscript. She has my thanks for her patience. My wife, Dottie, not only read over what I wrote, but claimed she enjoyed it. She said she has finally learned something about Freemasonry, and that every Mason's wife should read it!

Let's look at symbolism for a moment. We have become so familiar with this word in our daily lives we seldom think about it. The American flag is an excellent example. To many it's nothing but a piece of cloth colored red, white and blue. But the historian sees the thirteen original colonies in its stripes. The stars represent the number of present States. The patriot will see a glorious past and the flag as a symbol of loyalty. A Freemason sees all these things and more. The red becomes a symbol of the blood shed to create and preserve our country. The white symbolizes purity, and the establishment of freedom for all men. The blue takes on a symbol of fidelity to the highest principles. Actually, there is no limitation to what a person can find in this or any other symbol. Past experience, knowledge, and background help or hinder us in what we see.

So it is with Masonic symbolism. No one can ever write all there is to know about it. One can only state his personal views insofar as his perception helps him to see this symbolism. Consequently, this is not, and cannot be, the final word on the subject of Masonic symbolism. But I do hope the Master Mason will better understand the philosophy of Freemasonry after reading what is written on these pages.

Allen E. Roberts

July 4, 1973

Contents

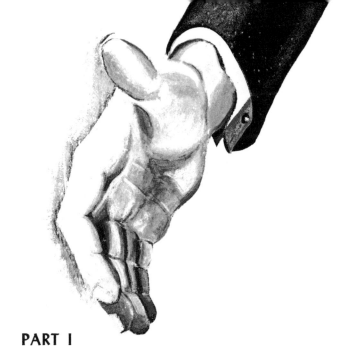

PART I

The Entered Apprentice Degree

"Let there be light!" the great Creator spoke,
And, at the summons, slumbering nature woke,
While from the east the primal morning broke,
  Back rolled the curtains of the night,
  And earth rejoiced to see the light.

* * * *

"Let there be light!" the Master's lips proclaimed,
And heart and hand unite in glad acclaim
To hail th' enrollment of a Brother's name,
  While he beholds with ravished sight
  The glories of the perfect light.

—Thomas W. Davis

And God said,
Let there be light;
and there was light.

Gen. 1:3

I

"Let There Be Light"

You have entered a new world. Symbolically and spiritually you have been reborn. This started the moment you were prepared to become a Freemason.

As you progress in Masonic knowledge your vision will broaden; you will become more vitally alive than ever before; you will become more aware of your fellowman, your family, your church and your country. Your whole philosophy of life will become richer.

This will take place, but only if you become Masonically educated.

The conferring of the three degrees in Freemasonry has made it possible for you to be a part of a world-wide Brotherhood. You were told that brothers will be found in every country in the world. You will find that this is true, even though Masonic lodges are not allowed to function under despotism. Freemasonry has always believed in the freedom of man. Where there is freedom, oppression cannot exist.

Because of this belief in individual freedom you will never be ordered to do anything in or for Freemasonry. You may be asked to serve on committees. You will be requested to attend the meetings of your lodge. You will be urged to learn more about the Craft than what is revealed in its ritual. You will find that the ritual is but the beginning of what can be a tremendous spiritual and philosophical experience.

There is much for you to discover in this new world you have entered. Yet, it is an old world, as you have been told. World-renowned men of this and preceding centuries were initiated much the same as you were. The changes in the ritual over the centuries have been fewer than we might expect. Freemasonry has always been careful to keep its work acceptable to all good men, regardless of their sect, country, religion, or opinion.

As you learn more about this ritual, the history of Freemasonry, its philosophy and its symbolism, you will grow within. As you grow within, it will be reflected outwardly in everything that you do.

You have learned that it was in your heart that you were first prepared to be a Freemason. Actually, it was your brain that did the preparing. The heart is but a symbol of what a man is or becomes; the brain does the work. But throughout the centuries the heart has been the favorite term of poets, writers, historians, and psalmists to describe man's feeling, his joy, his love, his disappointments, or sadness. Freemasonry has adopted this symbol and uses it repeatedly throughout its ritual.

To all people, educated or not, the heart is what the dictionary describes a symbol to be: "a sign by which one knows or infers a thing." Or, a symbol "stands for or suggests something else by reason of relationship, or convention"; "a visible sign of something invisible, as an idea, a quality."

You entered this world of symbolism immediately as an Entered Apprentice. Some of the symbolic lessons were explained to you as you progressed; others are explained later; some will never be taught. Some are virtually impossible to explain with words; they must come from the heart of the initiate himself. Then, there are symbols that have so many meanings that whole volumes can be written about them.

Teaching and learning through symbols has always been with us. For centuries man learned through pictorial symbols. Only a few men knew how to read and write. Then, late in the 14th Century Gutenberg helped make the printed word—letter symbols—available to even the lowliest of men. His invention of moveable type made this form of symbolism take on a world-wide uniformity.

Pictorial symbols have many meanings to different people. Consider the interpretations that can be put on the drawings of a sun, moon, lion, cow, or mule. By using the printed word an author has a greater opportunity of having his exact meaning understood. But even here he is in danger of being misunderstood. The 500 most commonly used words have over 15,000 different dictionary meanings!

Still, symbolism is all around us. With man's advancing knowledge came an enormous increase in the number of symbols he must understand if he is to survive. Every science, profession, craft, and even sport, has its symbolism. The musician would be lost without symbols; highway signs guide millions of us daily; the world of business would come to a standstill without its symbols; and we wouldn't know how

Bobby Fischer of America wrested the world chess championship from Boris Spassky of Russia if we didn't know the symbols of chess.

We are lost if we don't understand the symbols necessary to earn our livelihood. As Freemasons, we are lost if we don't understand the symbolism of the Order. Without knowing the meaning of the many symbols we cannot decipher the philosophy of Freemasonry.

Symbolism has kept Freemasonry a vital force in the world of fraternalism. Symbolism has set Masonry apart from all other organizations that would imitate her. Its method of teaching great truths through allegory and symbols has appealed to knowledgeable men throughout the ages. This method of teaching has helped Freemasons to satisfy their spiritual needs, and to accomplish what they "came here to do" —to improve themselves in Masonry.

Like millions who were initiated into Freemasonry before you, you were informed that your first duty is to improve yourself. In your search for truth, which is Masonry's most important quest, you will improve yourself. You will become more tolerant of the weaknesses of others. You will learn to love your fellowman more than ever.

You will be helped in your quest by God through prayer. You were told that you should attempt nothing of importance without first invoking the blessings of Deity. You, as a Freemason, have formed a partnership with God. It is a partnership that will assist you in accomplishing anything you attempt that has His approval.

You have learned that Freemasonry calls God "The Great Architect of the Universe." This is the Freemason's special name for God, because He is universal. He belongs to all men regardless of their religious persuasion. All wise men acknowledge His authority. In his private devotions a Mason will pray to Jehovah, Mohammed, Allah, Jesus, or the Deity of his choice. In a Masonic Lodge, however, the Mason will find the name of his Deity within the Great Architect of the Universe.

You undoubtedly have heard that Freemasonry is a "secret society" or it's "mysterious." A secret, or a mystery, is simply something that is unknown by the "outsider." The ritual, and the manner of initiation can be classed as a secret or a mystery. Everything else that is known about Masonry is available to all who are interested enough to read about the Craft. But there is much that is still unknown to even the ardent Masonic student. This is one reason there are Masonic Lodges of Research throughout the world.

You have heard your lodge referred to as a "Blue Lodge." Where blue came from to denote a Masonic lodge no one knows. There has been much speculation, though. The color blue has always been as-

GEORGE WASHINGTON AT PRAYER
Statue by Donald DeLue
Presented to Freedoms Foundation
at Valley Forge
By the Grand Lodge of Pennsylvania

sociated with what is deemed beneficial: chastity, fidelity, immortality, and prudence. The blue canopy of heaven is the covering of the Universal Lodge of Freemasonry. Blue has been adopted as the trim color for the aprons and jewel holders in many lodges. Purple is usually the color selected for the officers of the Grand Lodge. Numerous lodges, particularly in foreign countries, adopt combinations of colors and designs to set them apart. Actually, no one color can truly be used to describe Freemasonry. A Masonic lodge is a *Lodge*. It needs no color or adjective to describe it.

There are many definitions for Freemasonry. The one most widely used is: "Freemasonry is a beautiful system of morality, veiled in allegory and illustrated by symbols."

There are many who believe this definition is not accurate. Morality, as it pertains to the Craft, is not "veiled." It has been constantly described in the Monitors and other publications of various Grand Lodges. Morality has been covered at length by Masonic writers. It will be covered in several sections of this book. Allegory and symbols are veiled, as you will note as we go into them.

FREEMASONRY IS A WAY OF LIFE; AS AN ORGANIZATION, ITS PURPOSE IS TO MAKE GOOD MEN BETTER. You will find longer definitions of Masonry, but they will all come back to this brief statement. Throughout its long history, Freemasonry has been a way of life for millions of good men.

When did the history begin? No man knows. The oldest known Masonic document, the *Regius Poem,* was copied from older documents about 1390. Its modern spelling claims: "The Craft came into England, as I now say, / In the time of good King Athelstan's day." This would place Masonry in England about 526 A.D.

In the early years of the Grand Lodge of England, according to the best of historians, there were but two degrees. These consisted of Entered Apprentice and Fellow-Craft. Between 1725 and 1738 the Third, or Master Mason, Degree was added. All the business of a lodge was conducted in the First Degree. In Great Britain it still is; in the United States all business is conducted in the Master Mason, or Third, Degree.

You will learn that Freemasonry does not remain static. J. Hugo Tatsch, a Masonic historian, pointed this out in a recently discovered letter he wrote in 1935: "The more I delve in American Masonic History, the less dogmatic I become on all points involved. Our Masonry developed with the country, and in studying the subject, we must look upon it in the light of contemporaneous events and not by present day customs and standards. The structure of Freemasonry is con-

George Washington

b. Feb. 22, 1732
d. Dec. 14, 1799

Initiated Nov. 4, 1752
Fredericksburg, Va.

King Edward VII

Grand Master (England)
1874–1897

The design of the apron
has remained practically
unchanged through the
years

9

George Washington

1732–1799

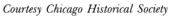

Benjamin Franklin

1706–1790

THE APRON PRESENTED TO WASHINGTON BY LAFAYETTE

In the Library of the Grand Lodge of Pennsylvania, F. & A. M., Philadelphia

stantly changing and it is to this fact that we owe its preservation. The principles are transmitted unimpaired, but the vehicle through which they are expressed changes as the years go on."

Tatsch has also pointed out why there must be a constant flow of new Masonic literature. Change is constant. New discoveries are made daily. The meaning of words change rapidly. An excellent example is the word "profane." Early Masonic writers used this word to describe a man who was not a Freemason. For many years this word has been associated with obscenity. How much better it is to say what we mean today—uninitiated, or "without the Temple." Then there can be no misunderstanding.

The same thing holds true of Freemasonry's symbols. While the symbols have remained the same, the words that describe them have changed. At times there has been something added or subtracted to give the symbol a deeper or unmistakable meaning.

One of these symbols, with which you are familiar, is the interlaced Square and Compasses—the "symbol of Freemasonry." This has been recognized and accepted as *the* Masonic emblem from the beginning of the 18th Century at least. The United States Patent Office took note of this in 1873. It told a flour manufacturer, and the world: "This device, so commonly worn and employed by Masons, has an established mystic significance, universally recognized as existing, whether comprehended by all or not, is not material to this issue. In view of the magnitude of the Masonic organization, it is impossible to divest its symbols, or at least this particular symbol—perhaps the best known of all—of its ordinary significance, wherever displayed." The manufacturer was denied the use of the Square and Compasses as a trade-mark.

It was about this time that some unknown "inventor" added a letter "G" in the center of the Square and Compasses. To many American Masons the emblem is not complete without this letter. This is not so in other countries, however. In other languages God does not start with the letter "G"; neither does Geometry.

This is but one of dozens of symbols that Freemasonry employs to imprint on the mind "wise and serious truths." Let's look at some that are indispensable to the ritual and meanings to be found in the First Degree Of Masonry.

2

Rebirth

Your preparation for your entrance into Freemasonry began the day your mother brought you into the world. It continued day by day and year by year.

During these years of preparation we have been guided by others wiser than ourselves. Our parents led us along paths in the unknown world step by step. Our teachers helped to enrich our minds with knowledge of the past and present. Our religious leaders aided us in understanding the rewards for living a good life.

All of these, and other associates, have been important. You know this now, if you didn't before. You have learned that Freemasonry accepts good men, then endeavors to make them better. You signified to the truth of this when you said that you were prepared in your heart to become a Freemason.

Your entrance into a lodge for initiation became, symbolically, your rebirth. All that becomes a part of this initiation strengthens this rebirth. Nothing is more beautiful, nothing more meaningful than this First Degree in Masonry. Nothing brings out more forcefully the elegance of the rebirth of man. The moral truth of Freemasonry becomes a masterpiece.

What we get out of Freemasonry starts with our rebirth—the initiation. What we end up with depends upon ourselves. Without question, we will receive more benefits than we contribute. We will get more out than we put in—not materially, but spiritually and mentally.

As we are prepared for initiation we quickly learn that we are a part of a world-wide Brotherhood. We are taking an important step in life. We are following in the footsteps of countless millions of good men. We are a part of a ritual of religious faith and ethical responsibility. We are to learn truths that have been hidden from us since we entered the world.

The cabletow symbolizes the tie you have to your new world. It can be visualized as not unlike the cord which unites the unborn child to its mother. Just as this cord is cut, to be replaced by love and care, so is the Masonic cord replaced by a stronger bond—the Mystic Tie of Brotherly Love. With the removal of the cabletow you have placed yourself under an obligation to Freemasonry. At the same time, because the rope has two ends, the Fraternity has placed itself under obligation to you. It has promised to train, teach, guide, and instruct you to be of more service to your fellowman as well as the Craft.

Something similar to a cabletow has been used in initiations as far back as recorded history goes. That a cord had a deep meaning is attested to by the Holy Bible. In I Kings 20:31–32, we learn that the King of Syria had been defeated in battle by Israelitish forces. The servants of the king "put ropes on their heads" and went before Ahab, King of Israel, to plead for the life of Ben-hadad. Their voluntary action and their pleas for mercy brought clemency for the vanquished king of Syria.

The cabletow acted as an outward, a visible pledge of submission and fidelity. It is the symbol of a vow to assist another, even at the risk of our lives. Its strength and length depend upon a man's ability to fulfill his obligations. It is a test of his character and his capacity to love.

How long is a cabletow? It's as long as you want it to be. It will reach as far as your moral principles go, or your material conditions will allow. Each man must be his own judge of the length of his cabletow. But if the cord of each Freemason were tied around the world, no earthly power could break the bond of brotherhood. It is truly the *Mystic Tie* that binds the Craftsmen together. This tie keeps Freemasonry a house undivided.

The lodge becomes a symbol of this new world to which you have been reborn. It is the world as it was thought to be. It's four-sided, with the sky as a canopy. It is symbolically all encompassing, extending from east to west and north to south as far as possible. It reaches from the surface to the center, and to the heavens. And Freemasonry can make this claim for the dimensions of a lodge, because Freemasons can be found everywhere. Masonry is a universal brotherhood.

A lodge is composed of all its members. A specific number must be present for it to be legally opened—seven for an Entered Apprentice Lodge, five for a Fellowcraft Lodge, three for a Lodge of Master Masons. Every lodge must have a Volume of the Sacred Law—the Holy Bible—square, compasses, and a Charter, or Warrant, from the Grand Lodge under whose jurisdiction it works.

In your preparation to enter the lodge you learned that worldly wealth and honors are not regarded as qualifications for your admission. This is demonstrated literally as well as symbolically. All evidence of what you acquired materially is left behind in the preparation room. You enter your new world with neither more nor less than the millions in whose footsteps you are following.

You learn that your entrance is not a mere opening of a door. It is accomplished by forms, ceremonies, actions, and words designed to impress upon your mind wise and serious truths. You know that this is not a frivolous event, but one of spiritual impressiveness.

Most of the forms and ceremonies of initiation are based on the truths that are found in the Holy Bible. This is apparent from the beginning. The Scriptual promise becomes an actuality: "Ask, and it shall be given you; seek and ye shall find; knock, and it shall be opened unto you." You asked for membership, because Freemasonry doesn't believe in solicitation. You sought admission of your own free will. After you had knocked, all that the Fraternity has to offer was opened before you.

The knocks which gained you admittance are symbolic of the freedom of man that Freemasonry teaches and exemplifies. You were free to ask for membership, or not to. You were free to stop anywhere along the way. You signified your freedom of choice when you knocked upon the door of your lodge. At the same time you demonstrated your determination to become a seeker of truth.

As no "great and important undertaking" should ever be taken "without first invoking the blessing of Deity," the knocks also symbolize a prayerful act. St. Luke 11:1–13 contains much of the meaning of your entrance into Masonry. It gives us a non-sectarian and universal prayer which begins, "Our Father, which art in heaven." It challenges us to practice Masonry's first tenet—Brotherly Love.

No candidate is permitted to bring anything of a metallic nature into a lodge. Freemasonry doesn't believe in violence. It's a law-abiding, peace-loving association. But this shouldn't be interpreted to mean that Masons are cowardly. On the contrary. They have been among the bravest when the honor of their country, their principles, or their integrity have been at stake. But the Freemason who has learned the teachings of the Craft will always seek a peaceful settlement of any dispute.

The divestation of objects that could be offensive symbolizes the peaceful nature of the Fraternity. It also symbolizes man's dependence upon his fellowman, as we will learn later.

We learn in the third chapter of Exodus that God said to Moses: "Put off thy shoes from off thy feet, for the place whereon thou standest is holy ground." In the Book of Ruth we are told: "Now this was the manner in former times in Israel concerning redeeming and concerning changing; for to confirm all things, a man plucked off his shoe, and gave it to his neighbor; and this was a testimony in Israel."

The removal of the shoes symbolizes humility (NOT humiliation). It signifies that meekness we all should display before a greater or supreme power. It proves to us that we are about to enter upon something that has not been defiled by anything unworthy. It tells us that we are to tread upon "holy ground." It sets the tone, not only for initiation, but for advancement in the degrees to follow.

The Rite of Discalceation, taken from the Latin, *discalceatus*, meaning "unshod," comes to Freemasonry from many sources, not only from the Bible. The custom was found in Ethiopia, Peru, and among the Druids. Pythagoras, of whom we will learn more later, told his followers to "offer sacrifices with thy shoes off."

In Freemasonry we find this Rite becomes two separate actions. By taking off both shoes we are signifying humility before God. It also symbolizes our faith in those with whom we are about to associate. It teaches us the need for cleanliness. Shoes protect the feet from injury as well as the filth in the outer world. We who walk "neither barefoot nor shod" are offering testimony that we have faith in the protection we will receive at the hands of our friends, that we are willing to humble ourselves before God and man and, to tread on hallowed ground, we must be clean.

The removal of one shoe becomes our second action. This is a symbol of our sincerity in the vow we take, an obligation to fulfill our duty to God and man. When we "pluck off our shoe" we are pledging upon our honor to be fair in our dealings. This can be compared to the swearing of our signature to a document before a Notary Public.

Your preparation to become an Entered Apprentice has taught you that you are to be reborn. This rebirth is spiritual and mental. Through Freemasonry's universal forms and ceremonies you are united with millions of men. These men have trod the same path as you and all others throughout many centuries. They have been judged, as will you, not by worldly wealth and honors, but by humility, faith, and sincerity.

"The Ancient of Days"
William Blake

Milton, in his Paradise Lost, Book VII, must have seen God
as the Supreme Geometer, when he wrote:
". . . . and in his hand
He took the golden compasses, prepared
In God's eternal store, to circumscribe
This Universe, and all created things.
One foot he centred, and the other turned
Round through the vast profundity obscure,
And said, 'Thus far extend, thus far thy bounds,
This be thy just circumference, O World!' "

3

Entrance

Into a strange and dark world you are guided to begin the
long journey to the truths that Freemasonry teaches. One of the first
lessons you learn is that man is dependent upon his fellowmen. From

19

the moment your mother gives you birth until the moment your coffin is lowered into your grave, you must depend on others.

The ritual explains part of the reason you participate in what is termed "circumambulation," which simply means "walking around." But it doesn't tell you that it was a part of the religious observances of ancient times. It links all Freemasons to the spiritual ceremonies of years gone by, as well as to all who have become Masons throughout the centuries. It symbolizes that homage that all of us owe to our God. It also is one of the many symbols of the dependence of man on man.

Throughout our lives we will meet with obstructions as we travel. Some will be minor, others major. If we are truly prepared in our particular endeavors, we will overcome them.

As King Solomon posted guards at the entrances to his temple, so must we. Our sentinels must keep us from having unworthy thoughts or deeds, from uttering words that will cause harm to ourselves or others. We must keep our consciences pure before God and man. The obstructions we meet, and guards we encounter, are symbolic of a pure mind, deeds, and action.

The 133rd Psalm, which is recited during the Initiatory Degree, can be said to symbolize unity. It can also be termed a symbol of Brotherly Love. Both are an essential need for that harmony which must prevail in every successful Masonic lodge. They are just as necessary for a happy life. This Psalm brings out the glories of unity and Freemasonry's first tenet.

The other two tenets, Relief and Truth, join Brotherly Love in a trio that brings out the best that man has to offer to the world.

Brotherly Love symbolizes the universality of man. It regards the whole human species as one family, regardless of race, religion, or creed.

Relief symbolizes man's duty. All men should feel duty-bound to aid, support, and be charitable to all who are in need. This does not mean, necessarily, the giving of money. There are many other ways to accomplish this "duty" as will be explained later.

Truth can be said to symbolize divinity. Truth is the foundation of everything that is just. It is what man is constantly seeking. But truth is impossible to define. All of us look at everything differently. We are conditioned by our environment, associates, and education. All of us look at life through restricted windows. No two people see exactly the same thing at the same time. What is factual to one, won't be to another. So, it is with symbolism. Each will see something different —and rightly so.

When we say we are seeking Masonic Light, we are actually saying we are seeking truth. Light, therefore, symbolizes truth. But light also symbolizes so many things no one can list them all. In the First Degree Masonic Light does symbolize charity, lawfulness, patriotism, reverence, and unselfishness, among other things.

That light is important, there can be no question. Without it life would soon cease to exist. It's so important that the first three verses in the Bible tell us: "In the beginning God created the heaven and the earth. And the earth was without form, and void; and darkness *was* upon the face of the deep. And the Spirit of God moved upon the face of the waters. And God said, Let there be light; and there was light." This was done on the first day of creation, demonstrating the need God felt for light.

Your brethren demonstrated the importance of light to you when they assisted in bringing you to Masonic Light. And you beheld the three Great Lights in Masonry. The representatives of the three Lesser Lights enabled you to see them.

You learned that the three Great Lights, insofar as Freemasonry is concerned, are the Holy Bible, Square and Compasses. The Holy Bible

RAYS OF LIGHT
The most prolific of all illustrators of the Bible was Gustaf Dore. None made a greater appeal than his original "And God said, Let There be Light." Here the figure of Jehovah has been removed to leave only the newly-created light to illumine the earth.

is God's gift to man. Within its pages can be found the truth that all Freemasons should seek. The Bible is also called the Volume of the Scared Law, because not only Christians and Jews can become Masons. Any good man who believes in Deity, by whatever name he may call Him, can petition for the degrees. Each religion has its own Volume of the Sacred Law. Unless a man takes his obligation upon the Volume of *his* law, his vows cannot be considered binding upon him.

Among other things, the Holy Bible (or the Koran for the Mohammedan, the Vedas for the Brahmin) symbolizes Truth, Faith, and

Hope. As the Volume of the Sacred Law, it proves Masonry's claim that men of all faiths, creeds, and races may travel the Masonic road together in harmony.

The Square symbolizes morality. It also is a symbol of righteousness. It keeps us in touch with God, for morality and righteousness cannot be separated from Him. Without all three the world would come apart. They set the standards for the Fraternity. Without standards the Fraternity would perish.

The Compasses symbolizes spirituality. It is interesting to note that the Compasses are symbolically hidden when you are first brought to light in Masonry. This signifies that man is hoodwinked by the senses

and must grope his way, slowly, from the darkness of ignorance to the light of truth. As the square cannot be corrected without a circle circumscribed by the compasses, man cannot find Divine truth outside the circle of law and love.

The most spiritual of all the working tools of Freemasonry is the Compasses. As an Entered Apprentice you are taught a valuable lesson. The Compasses should remind you to "circumscribe your desires and keep your passions within due bounds." And you are not to confine these duties to your brethren alone, but to all men.

As you advance to the next two degrees you find that the Compasses have further and deeper meanings. So do many of the other symbols you first encountered in your entrance into Masonry.

4

Forms and Ceremonies

You find that Freemasonry doesn't take its admonition lightly when it says that all undertakings should start with prayer. You also found that you were not alone in this great and important undertaking. You heard your brethren join in unison to say, "So Mote It Be."

So Mote It Be can be said to symbolize fellowship. It also signifies reverence. It links all Speculative Masons together. It joins them with the days of long ago. The phrase is no longer used except in Freemasonry, where it continues to be meaningful. *Mote* comes from an old Saxon word *motan* and is interpreted to mean "may or "might."

You soon learn that Freemasonry builds many of its great truths around the Temple of King Solomon. Much of its symbolism, legends, and allegory center around this magnificent shrine to God. This Temple has been a part of Speculative Masonry for so long that Masonry would die if the references to it were taken away. It is the link that binds the Speculative Craft to the operative masons of centuries ago. Of this

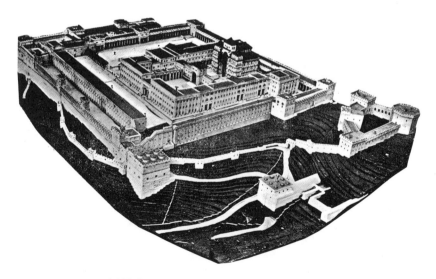

MODEL OF KING SOLOMON'S TEMPLE

25

you will learn more as you advance toward the degree of Master Mason.

Obstacles are a part of life. No man can strive toward any of his goals smoothly. When the waters are calm all of us can move forward easily. When storms strike, obstacles are thrown in our path. It takes courage to ride out the rough weather, or go around it so we can continue toward the goals we have set.

Obstacles give us an opportunity to analyze our strengths and our weaknesses. They help give us the courage of our convictions. They help us to realize that as human beings we are capable of making many errors. At the same time they give us the knowledge that we can rise above our errors; that we can surmount any obstacles thrown in our way. Obstacles, then, become a symbol of courage—courage to continue to work toward achieving our goals in life.

An "oblong square" appears to be a contradiction in terminology. A "square" has four equal sides; an "oblong" has two sides longer than the other two sides. This, of course, is a modern day description. It wasn't always so. Once they were called "perfect square" and "oblong square." A lengthy argument can be given for or against the term. But when we take into account the age of the symbolism of Freemasonry, we can accept "oblong square" without wincing like the purists. Both have four square corners, don't they?

At the time of the building of King Solomon's Temple the world was thought to have been oblong. A Masonic lodge is a representation of the then known habitable globe. A lodge symbolizes the world; an oblong square symbolizes a lodge. Take away the "oblong" and few lodges in the world can be termed a symbol of the world. Few are square; most are oblong.

The Entered Apprentice quickly learns that God, country, and all human beings are important to Freemasons. Nothing he does, no obligation he assumes, can or will transcend his duty to help, aid, and assist them at all times.

Obligation comes from the Latin *obligare,* meaning "to bind." An obligation becomes a binding force. In Freemasonry it unites its members with solemn promises, agreements, and covenants to be true to God and man.

An obligation shouldn't be confused with an oath. An obligation signifies promises and agreements made; an oath, such as "so help me God," made with the hand upon the Volume of the Sacred Law (usually the Holy Bible), is a vow to carry out the promises and agreements of the obligation. An oath is symbolic of the love (or fear) of God.

"Meanings are in people—not in words," states the script of a Masonic Leadership film on communication. So it has always been. To make certain a man understood the obligation he took, the same meaning was conveyed with two or three different words. Even today words don't mean the same to everyone. All of us look at life through "restricted windows." In the early days of the Craft, man's knowledge was much more restricted than today. The use of triads, or couplets, was most important.

Because of the age of Freemasonry and its ritual, several archaic words are to be found. One in particular gives us the most trouble. It is "Hele" and pronounced "hail," and shouldn't be confused with the pronunciation. "Hele" is from the Anglo-Saxon *helan* and means to cover, or conceal. So, in Freemasonry, when you promise to "hele" something, you promise to conceal it.

The first strictly Masonic symbols you behold are the Three Great Lights in Masonry. You find that these are the Holy Bible, Square and Compasses. All three of these belong to all men, but not as they are symbolized by Freemasonry. The Great Light in Masonry (the Holy Bible in this country) is opened upon the altar. Lying upon it are the other Great Lights—the Square and Compasses. Without all three no Masonic lodge can be legally open, nor could it exist. They are as necessary as is a Charter, or Warrant, from the Grand Lodge.

The Three Lesser Lights are also necessary. Without two of them, the sun and the moon, there would be no planet called "Earth." Without the third, the Worshipful Master, there could be no Masonic lodge. The latter is charged to emulate the first two. He should rule and govern his lodge as does the sun the day and the moon the night.

The penalty for the violation of your obligation appeared strange. It was. It is symbolic only. It has never been enforced. It never will be. In the Middle Ages, and before, religious beliefs were such that a man feared dying with an incomplete body. Such a body could not rise from the dead, it was thought. One that was buried in ground that

wasn't consecrated, as between high and low water mark, couldn't reach heaven. We know this isn't so.

There are penalties if you don't fulfill your Masonic obligations. They depend upon the degree of the violation. Reprimand in private or in open lodge, suspension, or expulsion are the penalties inflicted. These can come only after a fair trial in accordance with Grand Lodge

rules and regulations. But should you be guilty of un-Masonic conduct, even if known only to yourself, you will inflict an even greater penalty upon yourself. Your conscience will know no rest.

Symbolically, the covering of a lodge is the "Clouded Canopy or Starry Decked Heavens." This is the place where all good men hope to reach. This becomes the ultimate reward for striving for perfection. Freemasons are taught to use the visionary Ladder of Jacob to climb toward their reward.

The *three principal rounds* of Jacob's ladder are Faith, Hope, and Charity. Charity is now interpreted to mean "Love." The ritual informs us that "Faith may be lost in sight; Hope ends in fruition, but Charity extends beyond the grave throughout the boundless realms of eternity." If we use "Love" in place of "Charity" it brings the meaning of the ritual to life. Love is eternal; charity may end with the giving of alms.

But Masonic charity is in reality love. While it includes gifts of money, it is much more than that. More importantly, it is the giving of one's self. It's sympathy to the unfortunate and suffering; the tear for the widow; congratulations for the fortunate. Masonic charity symbolizes the heart of man.

The Ladder of Jacob has other rounds. Without them the three principal ones would be of little use in reaching Heaven. Among them are Brotherly Love, Relief, and Truth, the tenets of Freemasonry. To these should be added Temperance, Fortitude, Prudence, and Justice, the Cardinal Virtues of the Fraternity. Taken all together they symbolize perfection, something every Mason should strive to reach.

The tenets have been explained briefly. Whether they are called Brotherly Love, Relief, and Truth, or, as they are in some jurisdictions: Friendship, Morality, and Brotherly Love, they are important. All can be termed "Cardinal Virtues." Cardinal comes from the Latin *cardinalis,* meaning essential. The tenets are certainly essential to Freemasonry.

So are the four named Cardinal Virtues. Fortitude isn't mentioned as such in the Bible, but courage is. And courage is another word for fortitude. We can safely claim that Fortitude symbolizes courage. Fortitude, as used by Masons, doesn't refer to physical courage only. If it did, it would put this virtue on a level with limited intelligence. It refers to moral courage; the strength and ability to make a decision and stick to it regardless of the consequences. To maintain high principles, even if they may be unpopular for the moment. This is what the Masons who wore the blue and gray of opposing forces during the American Civil War did. And because they remembered to practice out

F   P   T   J

of their lodges what they had learned within, Freemasonry was strengthened. They practiced Fortitude.

Temperance symbolizes restraint. By practicing this virtue all Masons are required to place a restraint upon their passions and affections. They are charged to keep their minds free from the allurements of vice. Temperance, not merely in strong drink, but in *all* things, must be their aim.

Prudence is a symbol of wisdom. Anciently, it was wisdom that was a Cardinal Virtue. Changing it to Prudence doesn't change its nature. You will find that Freemasonry teaches the necessity of acquiring wisdom. Wisdom of mind, heart, and soul. Wisdom comes from thinking, not just from education. It is something that brings man closer to his Creator. With wisdom comes knowledge, love, and truth.

Justice, as it is practiced Masonically, symbolizes equality. Justice is usually pictured as a blindfolded woman holding scales and a sword. But this is far removed from what Masonic justice should be. Man should govern his own actions, openly and not blindfolded. His conduct toward others should not be aggressive. He should do what he does because he really wants to, not because he is forced to. The justice of a Freemason should be unselfish and self-sacrificing.

Another term you were taught was unfamiliar. It's called a *Due Guard.* You were taught to use it as a form of salutation, because it is a symbol of respect. It also calls upon you always to remember your obligation as an Entered Apprentice. By using it before the Master and Wardens of the lodge, you have signified your agreement to submit to their authority. The name may have come from the French *Dieu Garde,* meaning "God guard me."

It has been said that there are three great religious rites in Masonry. Two of them, the Rite of Discalceation, barefoot before God, and the

Rite of Circumambulation, going around an altar from east to west by way of the south, have been explained briefly. The third is the Rite of Investiture, or Purification. This takes place when you are presented with a lambskin or white leather apron.

So that you might have something with which to compare the value of your apron, you were told something of its antiquity. It is "more ancient than the Golden Fleece or Roman Eagle." The Order of the Golden Fleece was founded in 1429. The Roman Eagle was Rome's ensign a century before the Christian era. Your apron is more "honorable than the Star and Garter." The Order of the Star was created in the middle of the Fourteenth Century; the Order of the Garter was founded in England in 1349. But it will only be more honorable if it is worthily worn. You have proven your right to wear it by being tried and tested. You must continue to prove you are worthy of wearing it by putting into practice the lessons, teachings, and philosophy of the Order.

As a badge of antiquity, your apron puts emphasis on the value of the past, and its contribution to the present and future happiness of man. The symbolism of your apron has come out of the mists of time. It has been tested by men of religion as well as laboring men. As it was worn with honor by the operative mason, so must it be today by the Speculative Mason.

The apron, among many things, is a symbol of Innocence, Purity, and Honor. In ancient times it was a badge of distinction. None but superior members of the Jewish priesthood could wear one. It is still a badge of distinction. Not all men are permitted to wear the Masonic apron.

The Ornaments of a Lodge are the Mosaic Pavement, Indented Tessel, and Blazing Star. The black and white of the mosaic pavement symbolize good and evil, or the contrast of any opposites. What the

significance of the Indented Tessel and Blazing Star may have been is unknown. None of the old rituals mention them. They aren't mentioned in the Bible. It may be assumed that the Blazing Star symbolizes Deity; the border is symbolic of fellowship, or the binding together of man with God.

The three "burning tapers" in a lodge are symbolic of the sun, moon, and Worshipful Master. Each is a governing body. The sun governs the day, the moon the night, and the Master his lodge.

You were told that every regular and well-governed lodge has six jewels as part of its furnishings. Three of these are movable; three immovable. They aren't precious stones. They're called jewels because of their value to the operative builders and because they're symbols of morality for Speculative Masons.

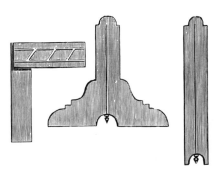

The jewels considered immovable (in America) are the Square, Level, and Plumb. Replicas of these are worn by the three stationed officers of the lodge. The Square is worn by the Master and symbolizes morality; the Level by the Senior Warden is a symbol of equality; the Plumb by the Junior Warden symbolizes an upright life.

A question asked many times is: "Why are these jewels considered immovable?" The officers who wear them don't remain stationary. They do move about during the conferring of degrees. They are considered "immovable" because each is assigned to a specific officer of the lodge. Every lodge must have a Master and two Wardens present or it can't be legally opened. In this sense, the Square, Level, and Plumb are immovable. As far as the Mason is concerned, the symbolism of these jewels should be fixed in the heart and never removed.

The movable jewels—the Rough Ashlar, the Perfect Ashlar, and the Trestle (or Tracing) Board—may be absent from a lodge and it still may be opened legally. They do teach moral lessons, however, and should be present in every lodge. The Rough Ashlar is a crude stone, just as it's taken from the quarry. It symbolizes the uneducated man, the man unaware of his potential in the Fraternity.

The Perfect Ashlar is a symbol of the educated man, the man who has been taught by those more knowledgeable than himself in the principles of Masonry. As an object in the lodge it is a stone that has been squared and tested by the tools of the Entered Apprentice and

The Legend of King Solomon and the Iron Worker

34

Fellowcraft. The Trestle Board, used by the master workman to draw his designs upon, is a symbol of perfection. It is symbolically a spiritual board on which a man should lay out his plans to build his "living stones" into a Temple to the Great Architect of the Universe.

When Freemasons stopped dedicating their lodges to King Solomon is not known. Nor do we know the reason this was changed. In 1598 is found the first reference to St. John the Evangelist as a patron. Why not St. Thomas, the patron saint of architecture and building? No one knows.

Reproduced by permission of Acacia Mutual Life Insurance Co., Washington, D. C.

Shown above is President George Washington, in full Masonic regalia and surrounded by brother Master Masons, laying the cornerstone of the United States Capitol Building on September 18, 1793. It is believed that during these ceremonies he used the square and level to lay the stone according to traditional Masonic rites. This cornerstone laying is one of the most important events in the history of Masonry in the United States. The original was painted by Stanley M. Arthurs, F.A.A.M. *and is the property of the Acacia Mutual Life Insurance Company.*

Two pagan ceremonies continued to remain popular well into the third century of the Christian era. These were the summer and winter solstices. The Church decided to take them into its bosom and gave them new names. St. John's Day in summer, and St. John's Day in winter were born. The Baptist's Day is celebrated on June 24; the Evangelist's on December 27. And even today in many parts of the country, these days are celebrated by Freemasons.

There never was a "Lodge of the Holy Sts. John of Jerusalem." Symbolically, though, every Freemason comes from this Lodge. It symbolizes the ideal which all of us should strive to reach. Using this phrase as a starting point for your Masonic career means that you are dedicated to the principles those men stood for. One was learned, the other zealous. Both were godly. Each had virtues that enhanced the other.

You could not have helped but to be thrilled and full of pride when you reached the Northeast Corner of the lodge. There you stood a just and upright Mason! Every brother present exulted with you. You were about to complete the first step of the most meaningful journey of your life.

The Northeast Corner! That's where the first stone of a public building is usually laid. That's where the cornerstone of every Masonic

life is laid. With it comes rejoicing. Stones and mortar will decay and rot away. The spiritual cornerstone, which is you, is eternal. But for this one time only you stand there in the Northeast as a symbol of a beginning—a new Masonic life.

This had to bring into focus that moment when you represented a Point Within a Circle, bordered by two perfect parallel lines and the Volume of the Sacred Law. You were told that the lines represented the two Sts. John, and that you should keep yourself circumscribed within the precepts of the Holy Bible.

The symbolism of the Point Within the Circle has come down to us from time immemorial. No building can be properly built without an accurate square. Our operative brethren used the point to construct the circle. The square was tested for squareness by using a diameter and a point on the circle. The knowledge of how to test a square for accuracy was the great secret of the master builder. The great secret of the Speculative Mason is the knowledge of how to use the teachings of the Craft to build a Spiritual Temple so that it will stand the test of time. This symbol becomes a test of our virtue.

You learned, perhaps for the first time in your life, what it means to be actually destitute. You could not produce even a simple object to attest to your initiation. You must have felt bewildered and embarrassed. It was a lesson you, and those who have preceded you, will never forget. Those who seek your aid will find it willingly given, if it's in your power to give it. But you must remember, money is not necessarily what is needed. It could be merely a kind word, a hearty clasp of the hand, a pat on the back, or a smile.

The Rite of Destitution is symbolic of compassion.

The Working Tools of an Entered Apprentice are the Twenty-four Inch Gauge and Common Gavel. The Gauge is a symbol of purpose or time; the gavel is symbolic of power.

To all men, time is all important. A wasted minute can't be retrieved. A minute is precious. Time must be used productively, or nothing can be accomplished. The man who wastes his own time or that of another squanders away something he can't replace.

The ritual tells us that Freemasons should spend eight hours serving

God and those in distress; eight hours for work; and eight for refreshment and sleep. Here there is proof, again, that Freemasonry was far ahead of its time. This ritual was written long before the eight hour work day, at a time when man worked from twelve to sixteen hours, six days a week. You will note, too, that two-thirds of a Freemason's time is to be spent in service and work.

The Common Gavel, the ritual informs us, should be used to fit our minds "as living stones for that Spiritual Building—that House not made with hands—eternal in the Heavens." It's a powerful instrument. When used for power alone it can be destructive. But power that is channeled toward good purposes will result in constructive achievement. The latter is the manner in which you, as a Mason, should use the power that God gives you.

Chalk, Charcoal, and Clay you were told are symbolic of freedom, fervency, and zeal. The Entered Apprentice will serve his apprenticeship with work and study, of his own free will and accord. He will do so with fervency, eager in his desire to do good work. His zeal will help him prove he wants to become a "living stone" in the Temple of Freemasonry.

In the early days of Speculative Masonry the symbols of the Craft were drawn on the floor of the building in which the lodge was meeting. Chalk or charcoal were the instruments used. The candidate had these symbols pointed out to him as he progressed through the degree. When the lodge was over, the tiler or candidate erased these "secret" symbols with a mop and a bucket of water. But when the lodge met on "high hills" or "low vales," earth became the carpet for the drawings; a hoe or rake the "eraser."

It is obvious that once chalk and charcoal were necessary to "draw the lodge." When floor cloths, and later wall charts, were used, an explanation became necessary for these three items. So, they were given the spiritual symbolism of freedom, fervency, and zeal.

By practicing these three, you will have become ready to receive further light in Masonry. You will move from youth to manhood. From an Entered Apprentice to a Fellowcraft.

PART II

The Fellowcraft Degree

But I am given strength and skill
   To do the work assigned to me;
Whate'er my task, it is God's will
   That I perform it worthily,
A living stone make fit to grace
   The Temple's walls, and help them rise—
Although it fill but humble place—
   A little nearer to the skies.

—George H. Free

I

Reaching for Manhood

In all ages, in all countries, in many religions, when a youth reaches the years of manhood there is rejoicing. In many places and religions there are elaborate ceremonies and rituals that usher in this happy event. The *bar mitzvah* of the Jewish religion is perhaps the best known ceremony today.

You, an Entered Apprentice, have symbolically served your seven-year apprenticeship as a craftsman. You are about to deliver up your "masterpiece" to be judged by your superiors. You are about to enter the second phase of your training.

What you received and learned as an Entered Apprentice is symbolic of youth. The ceremonies you pass through, and what you will learn as a Fellowcraft will be symbolic of manhood. It will be a manhood of continuing education.

You have proved your worth to your instructor since you received the First Degree. He has vouched for you to the Master and Wardens of your lodge. So, you, as a brother, entered a Lodge of Entered Apprentices and witnessed the opening ceremonies for the first time. You were permitted to participate in a ritual that is centuries old.

As time goes on you will learn that the opening and closing ceremonies of a lodge serve to remind us of our obligations. They bring out the solemnity, the beauty, and the spirituality that is Freemasonry. Because you participate, along with the officers and others present, you will be continually reminded that you are a vital part of the Fraternity.

You were undoubtedly nervous when you were called upon to prove to your brethren that you were worthy of advancement. But as the ancient phrases and words of the ritual you had learned came readily, your nervousness disappeared. You realized, too, that your brethren were with you. Silently, they were cheering you on. After your "master-piece" had been presented for the acceptance or rejection of the members, you participated in the closing ceremonies.

The Stewards weren't long in letting you know you had been accepted. They prepared you in much the same manner as they had before. One great difference you note is that you're no longer a candidate—you're a brother! Because of this, the cabletow isn't a restraining force; it's a strengthening force. It's a signal to go to work for Freemasonry and the human race.

Your obligation, you realize, is broader. Earlier, the need for secrecy was stressed strongly. As a Fellowcraft, the needs of your fellowman become even more important. You can no longer think of yourself merely as an individual, but as a small part of a much greater whole. The area encompassed by your promises covers the duties of a man who believes in God. These duties shouldn't be confined only to Freemasons, but to all good men.

"Light from God"

Darkness, in all forms of initiation, has always symbolized ignorance. It is necessary for the heart to receive those truths that are taught. Often this can be best accomplished before the eye beholds the distractions that are always present. The "hoodwink" is a symbol of ignorance, with knowledge to come with light. Without darkness you wouldn't appreciate the light. The appreciation of Masonic light is made meaningful. It comes through quoting God. "Let there be light," said God—and there was light! And you receive this light with the wholehearted assistance of your brethren. You find this comforting. It's a continuation of the First Degree.

You find that the Square has yet another meaning. It stands for Virtue. Virtue should guide you in all your transactions with your fellowman. No man who cheats or defrauds another can be a Freemason in his heart. He may be able to hide his actions from man, but he can't from God.

The Square, as one of the Working Tools of a Fellowcraft, has another virtue added—Morality. Although in some quarters the word "square" has become a term of contempt, to the right-thinking man it still has a moral and virtuous significance. When you "act upon the square," you are telling the truth, as you see it. You are giving the other fellow an "honest deal."

A question often asked is, "What is morality?" It is difficult to define. What is moral to one man may be immoral to another. Each man must decide for himself what the word encompasses, taking into account the moral standards of the society in which he lives. He must take into account his conscience, circumstances, and conduct. He must set his own standards, his own principles. It can be dangerous to apply his standards in judging another person. Which brings us to another of the Working Tools of a Fellowcraft.

The Plumb was used, and still is, by operative masons to test perpendiculars. It's unlikely that any wall will stand for long if it isn't straight. It's highly unlikely that a Mason who doesn't lead an upright life can be of any help to his fellowman. He certainly won't enhance the Fraternity in the community in which he lives. The Freemason who will follow the quest for truth will understand the symbolism of the Plumb. It stands for righteousness—an upright life before God and man. It becomes a standard by which to test morality. By understanding this symbol, the Mason can put into practice the meaning of the other Working Tools.

The Level is used to prove horizontals in operative masonry. It's used by the Speculative Mason as a symbol of Equality. The equality of man before God was pictured and practiced by Freemasonry long before it became popular in other circles. Masons meet upon the level. They have the same duties, responsibilities, and rights. They have the same Almighty Parent. They are brothers.

Equality doesn't mean, and never did, that all men have the same skills or abilities. All men are first of all individuals. It is this individuality that makes Freemasonry great. Individuality builds countries, communities, businesses. It creates wealth or depression. It brings peace or war, which indicates that it is dependent upon the teachings received in youth and early manhood.

Freemasonry in its formative years endeavored to create a level, a universal brotherhood where men could achieve mutual respect and understanding. Where they could work in peace and harmony. They achieved this goal! They kept out of the lodge those things that divide men—religion, politics, nations. Regardless of a Mason's political beliefs, his religion, or nationality, he can meet upon the level with his brethren in a Masonic lodge.

Symbolically, you will be building a Spiritual Temple. It will require hard labor. Just to construct the level site for its foundation will require

thorough spiritual work. Your horizontal platform will provide the stage from which you will realize an understanding of all men as equal before God. Your work will be rewarded. You will receive the approval of the Supreme Architect of the Universe, if it is Level, Plumb, and Square work.

The Fellowcraft is symbolically and factually a builder. He is presented with builder's tools. He is urged to build square, level, and plumb. And he must keep building if he is to become a part of the great heritage left him by his forefathers of the operative craft.

You were told something of the early days of architecture. You learned that from crude beginnings the operative mason continued to grow in knowledge and skill. His first efforts provided rough, low walls to protect himself and family from rain and wind. From there he went on to build higher walls and bind the stones with cement. Later he learned to cover them with existing material. Gradually, he found the means to erect stately cathedrals, castles, and other large buildings. Many of them stand today as a testimony to his craftsmanship.

While the operative masons were developing their craftsmanship, they instituted a high degree of morality. They learned to protect their principles and their secrets through the use of a simple ritual. As the years went by, the ritual became more sophisticated. But throughout the years tools and implements of architecture were used symbolically to imprint wise and serious truths upon the mind.

In the Seventeenth Century, if not before, nonoperative men were accepted into some of the lodges, or guilds, of masons. They accepted the teachings of morality laid out by their operative brethren. Because most of these "accepted masons" were learned men, it is likely they expanded the symbolism of the rituals then in use. And there were many different rituals being used. However, they were in several respects similar.

Operative masonry gave way to Speculative Masonry in 1717. That's when the first Grand Lodge was formed in London, England. The old rituals that could be found were gathered together. Dr. James Anderson, a Presbyterian minister and Scotsman, was commissioned to use them as a basis for Constitutions to govern all Freemasons. Anderson's *Constitutions of 1723* is still the basis for all Masonic law.

Even in the pre-Grand Lodge rituals are found references to those two great pillars you encountered. Their symbolism then, as now, was the same. Boaz signified Strength; Jachin, Establishment. God promised David that He would establish His Kingdom in Strength.

Boaz, the right hand pillar, can also symbolize power; Jachin, choice or control. In the process of becoming a Fellowcraft you passed be-

THE
CONSTITUTIONS
OF THE
FREE-MASONS

CONTAINING THE

History, Charges, Regulations, &c.
of that moſt Ancient and Right
Worſhipful *FRATERNITY.*

For the Uſe of the LODGES.

L O N D O N:

Printed by WILLIAM HUNTER, for JOHN SENEX at the *Globe,*
and JOHN HOOKE at the *Flower-de-luce* over-againſt *St. Dunſtan's*
Church, in *Fleet-ſtreet.*

In the Year of Maſonry —— 5723
Anno Domini —— —— 1723

tween these pillars of your own free will. This signified that you are
no longer a youth, but a man. You now have the essentials for success,
achievement, and happiness.

If you passed these pillars with understanding, if you realize that
power without control is dangerous, you have learned the lesson
taught by the symbolism of the pillars. You are ready to begin your
journey up the Winding Stairs to the Middle Chamber.

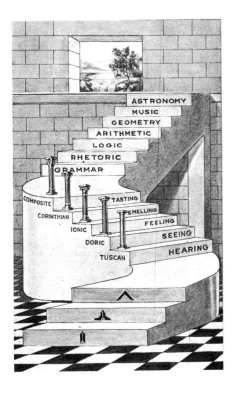

2

Into the Unknown

Before starting this journey into the unknown, a further examination of the two great pillars should be made. There have been many contradictions about their size, decorations, and everything else about them. Flavius Josephus, a First Century A.D. Jewish historian, covered the early history of the Jews. Among the things he had to say about the building of King Solomon's Temple was this:

Now Solomon sent for an artificer out of Tyre, whose name was *Hiram*. He was by birth of the tribe of Naphtali, on the mother's side (for she was of that tribe), but his father was Ur, of the stock of the Israelites. This man was skillful in all sorts of work; but his chief skill lay in working in gold, and silver, and brass, by whom were made all the mechanical works about the temple, according to the will of Solomon. Moreover this Hiram made two hollow pillars,

49

whose outsides were of brass, and the thickness of the brass was four fingers breadth, and the height of the pillars was eighteen cubits, and their circumference twelve cubits; but there was cast, with each of their chapiters, lily-work that stood upon the pillar, and it was elevated five cubits, round about which there was net-work interwoven with small palms made of brass, and covered the lily-work. To this also were hung two hundred pomegranates in two rows. The one of these pillars he set at the entrance of the porch on the right hand, and called it *Jachin,* and the other at the left hand, and called it *Boaz.*

What's the length of a cubit? There's much honest disagreement. Depending on the source referred to, it can be anywhere from thirteen to twenty-four inches. It is considered to be the length of the forearm

One artist's conception of the Porch of King Solomon's Temple showing the bowl-like containers at the tops of the Pillars

from the elbow to the tip of the middle finger. But it doesn't matter. You can do what E. G. Howland and Dr. Paul Leslie Garber did. They reconstructed the Temple accurately from Biblical and other accounts. They used a scale of ⅜″ to the cubit. They ended up with a model that measured 15″ from the court pavement to the top of the cornice.

Were the chapiters surmounted by two globes termed Celestial and Terrestrial? Not exactly. They could have been two bowl-like containers in which to burn incense. Early illustrations of the reconstruction of Solomon's Temple showed the chapiters as bulbous protuberances, probably derived from the lotus (lily) bud. The early ritualists could have mistaken these for spheres. Symbolically, however, they can be considered globes. And they can stand for the universality of Freemasonry.

The lily-work, you were told, symbolizes peace, something the Freemason should always work for. The pomegranates denote plenty; the net-work, unity.

You began your symbolic journey to the Middle Chamber by climbing three steps. These were representative of the three Stationed Officers of the lodge, the Worshipful Master, Senior and Junior Wardens. This assured you that you were not traveling alone. You were being assisted by the Craft everywhere. Then, too, you had God with you. Three is symbolic of Deity. You have become a vital part of the Mystic Tie that is Freemasonry.

The five steps are symbolic of the Fellowcraft Degree as a whole. It takes five to hold a Fellowcraft's Lodge; there are five Orders of Architecture; Geometry is the fifth science; there are five Human

THE FIVE ORDERS OF ARCHITECTURE
Tuscan   Doric   Ionic   Corinthian   Composite

Senses, and so on. But the points that were stressed to you were their representation of the orders of architecture and the human senses.

You learned that the Doric, Ionic, and Corinthian were the original orders of architecture. These were invented by the Greeks. The Romans added two, the Tuscan and the Composite. But there must be much more than pillars in the art of architecture. Buildings are erected stone by stone. The stones must be chipped away until they are suitable for use. Properly mixed cement must be used to hold them together. But first of all there must be a plan, a goal to reach for.

The symbolism is evident. There are five orders of architecture, signifying there are many plans a man may follow to build his Spiritual Temple. You are free to select your goals without any interference from Masonry. But Masonry does want you to choose wisely. Don't build aimlessly.

Freemasonry is a well-rounded plan for living. Without the five senses, a man couldn't live as a man. He couldn't plan. He couldn't learn. He can get along without one or two, provided he makes those that are left more sensitive.

But there is another factor that helps man use his senses in his relations with life. That's his mind, or soul, or spirit. Through his mind and senses man acquires knowledge. Through them he seeks education. And it's the seeking of knowledge and education that is stressed throughout the Fellowcraft Degree.

You are taught that the seven Liberal Arts and Sciences are Grammar, Rhetoric, Logic, Arithmetic, Geometry, Music, and Astronomy. All of these, and more, the Mason should understand. But Masonry stresses the need for knowledge in the fifth science—Geometry. In the Seventeenth Century these studies were regarded as the basic curriculum of a liberal education. Concepts have changed. Astronomy is interrelated with mathematics and physics. Other sciences such as electricity, chemistry, and biology were unknown when the Masonic ritual was born.

Because the ritual has remained the same doesn't mean that you should. You must grow. You can't stand still. Why not consider all

methods of communication as a part of Rhetoric and Grammar? Logic, a method of reasoning? Arithmetic and Geometry visualized as all science? Music as all sweet and harmonious sound, all poetry, beauty, art, nature? Astronomy, a study of all that's beyond earth? Taken all together, the practice of the truest brotherhood?

Man's greatest virtue is his courage. It takes courage to face the unknown. A straight stairway can be climbed with an easy mind. You can see what's ahead. Not so with a winding stairway. You can't tell what's just around the bend. The Winding Stairs you travel to the Middle Chamber are symbolic of life. We don't know what lies ahead. Each individual must climb his own stairway to his destiny. Seldom will the way be straight.

Man will always climb because he has courage. His faith will lead him upward. He will earn his wages and receive them in some Middle Chamber of life.

You were told that a symbol of Plenty was "a sheaf of wheat or ear of corn suspended at or near a waterford—or waterfall." The "corn" mentioned in the Bible isn't the corn known in this country today. It was wheat, barley, or some other grain, called corn in other countries. There is a long standing argument (which we'll not enter!) as to exactly what *Shibboleth* means.

The Bible merely explains that *Shibboleth* was a test of pronunciation, a pass-word. It tells us that during a war between the Ephraimites and the men of Gilead, "the Gileadites took the passages of Jordan before the Ephraimites." When a man asked permission to cross the river, a Gileadite asked, "Art thou an Ephraimite? If he said, Nay: Then said they unto him, Say now Shibboleth: and he said Sibboleth; for he could not frame to pronounce it right. Then they took him, and slew him at the passages of Jordan." It is interesting to note "passages" is mentioned twice.

The obstructions you encountered signify your courage, your willingness, your ability to join with your brethren spiritually. You have demonstrated your worthiness to be admitted into the places which Freemasonry considers the highest and most sacred in the temple of the Order.

You received wages as a Fellowcraft that are paid no more. In ancient days, though, corn, wine, and oil were wealth. They were used instead of money. Grapes in the vineyard were turned into skins of wine. Olives became cruses of oil. These, together with bushels of corn, were the dollars and cents of today.

An ear of grain (corn) has been a symbol of plenty since the beginnings of mythology. Our cereals today take the name from Ceres, goddess of abundance. Corn is also a symbol of nourishment.

The symbolism for wine comes from the "Feast of Booths," which took place in the early fall. It was a time of joy and gladness. The newly pressed juice of the grape was enjoyed by all. It was a symbol of refreshment.

The importance of the oil of the olive to those of bygone years should not be underestimated. It served not only as food and for lighting purposes, but as an anointment or perfume when suitably mixed with spices. It was a symbol of joy and gladness. It provided wealth, jobs, and security to many. A good crop brought happiness to untold numbers of people.

Together, the wages of a Fellowcraft must symbolize industry. If you had not worked to put together your "masterpiece" (the catechism or lecture of the First Degree), if you had not learned as you traveled up the Winding Stairs, if you had not successfully surmounted the obstacles along your journey, you would not have been rewarded. You did receive your corn, wine, and oil. You were recognized as worthy of being called a Fellow of the Craft.

The Jewels of a Fellowcraft are the Attentive Ear, Instructive Tongue, and Faithful Breast. In the art of communication—conveying information from one person or group to another person or group—the ability to listen properly is difficult indeed. Listening, strange as it may seem, is one of the most important steps in communicating effectively. The developers of the Masonic ritual, realizing this importance, made it one of the Jewels of a Fellowcraft. They knew that an Attentive Ear was a necessity if the lessons Freemasonry teach were to be transmitted "pure and unimpaired" from generation to generation. The life of Freemasonry absolutely depends upon ears that are *attentive*.

An Instructive Tongue is also a necessity. The passing on of the ritual is done from "mouth to ear." And the tongue must be *instructive*. The knowledge conveyed must be accurate. If it isn't, errors will be passed on to untold numbers of recipients.

But the tongue should pass on more than ritual. It must inform Masons about the great truths contained within the system of Freemasonry. Its history, philosophy, and symbolism, when understood, will make all men better. But, again, the qualifying word, *Instructive*, must be emphasized.

The Faithful Breast, symbolically, receives the information from the Instructive Tongue through the Attentive Ear (it's actually locked within the brain). Nothing transmitted and received in confidence will escape from the *Faithful* Breast. It becomes a repository for those few actual secrets you are entrusted with as you progress through the three degrees of Masonry. It also becomes a holding place for the Masonic ideals you should impart to your brethren to help them grow into better men.

You were informed that the letter "G," which you found suspended over the chair of the Worshipful Master, alludes to Geometry, the fifth science. It is there for all to see, symbolizing the faith and fellowship you enjoy while the lodge is open. Geometry is considered the "thought form" of God in nature. It does reveal to us many of the beauties created by the Supreme Architect.

So, it comes as no surprise to you to learn that "G" is also the initial of the sacred name of Deity. And because Masonry teaches through symbolism, by an indirect way, God is frequently called the Great Architect of the Universe. Masons believe in God so strongly and deeply they don't pronounce His name carelessly. They don't want to lose the awe of God. Masons walk in His presence constantly. But it's impossible not to feel a little closer to Him in the lodge with the letter "G" ever shining in the East.

As a Fellowcraft, you are symbolically and Masonically a builder. You have been presented with builders' tools. You have been taught to build your life square, level, and plumb. While this was said earlier, it is worth repeating. At the beginning you were an Apprentice striving to reach this goal.

You have been taught the value of work. You know the importance of acquiring knowledge. But knowledge merely acquired and hoarded is of little value. It is in sharing it with others that it gains its worth. It is this sharing that will make you richer as a Builder and in the sight of God.

You have become a Perfect Ashlar ready for the builder's use. The Builder is the Great Architect of the Universe; the building is your Spiritual Temple. May you grow in knowledge and wisdom, as befits a builder of that "house not made with hands." May you truly earn the wages of a Fellow of the Craft so that you may deserve Master's wages.

PART III

The Master Mason Degree

Let us then be forging, forging stronger still the Mystic chain,
For the glory of the meeting and the work that doth remain.
In the spirit of the Poet,[1] let us do our work with care
"As we meet upon the Level, and we part upon the Square."

—L. B. Mitchell

[1] Rob Morris

59

I

Toward the Summit

After what must have appeared to you to be a long time, you reached the moment you were waiting for. You were ready to start your climb to the pinnacle of Freemasonry. You were about to receive the Sublime Degree of Master Mason.

The Third, or Master Mason, Degree *is* the pinnacle of Freemasonry. There is none higher. True, there are degrees with higher numbers. There are many, many other degrees that have attached themselves to Freemasonry. But none of these could exist without lodges of Master Masons. Membership in these branches is predicated upon a man's remaining a Master Mason in good standing.

While there can be no solicitation for members of a lodge, this isn't so for the appendant bodies. You will probably be urged to join one or more of them quickly. Many jurisdictions have no "waiting period" before you can be solicited. The wise Master Mason will wait, though, until he has a firm foundation of experience in the lodge. He will then make a better and more knowledgeable member for the appendant body, as well as for the lodge.

As a Master Mason, many doors will be opened to you. You will be eligible to visit any lodge in the world, if its Grand Lodge is recognized by your Grand Lodge. Your Grand Secretary can tell you if it is or isn't. Through this you will find friends and brothers almost everywhere you travel.

There are many honors that can come to you as a Master Mason, if you are worthy of them.

Actually, serving your fellowman should be reward enough for all of us. Nothing can really bring greater satisfaction. You have promised, as have all who preceded you and those who will follow, to serve God and man. And there is no joy greater than seeing one you have helped along the way become a success. For you to be truly helpful, you need all the "Light" you can obtain.

More Light (or Further Light) in Masonry is what you tell the Worshipful Master you most desire. To impress this fact on your mind it's mentioned four times, and you repeat it once in each degree. As has been said, when you seek light you are trying to discover truth.

Your preparation for this search, you find, is much the same as before. The Cabletow, this time, symbolizes how strongly you are now united with the Craft, and the Craft with you. Your ties, obligations, duties, and responsibilities have increased considerably, now that you're about to become a Master Mason. These will stay with you for the balance of your life.

In the Entered Apprentice Degree the foundation for the building of your Spiritual Temple was laid. The framework was added according to age-old plans and designs. In this, the Master Mason Degree, you will receive lessons and teachings that are meant to be everlasting. They will be stored within your Temple to be used now and throughout your life.

The symbols you have been taught in the first two degrees concern themselves with the tools and emblems of architecture. Their symbolic meanings have laid the foundation for greater lessons and symbolism. These concern your soul. They cover life with its triumphs and its tragedies. Although they can't fully cover all the lessons to be taught, they become a guide—a plan of life—you can safely follow.

A great drama is the climax of the Master Mason Degree. You will return to it continuously for inspiration and help. You will find comfort in its truths, not only in the lodge, but in your everyday pursuits. Spiritually, you will reach full manhood.

There are many forms of Masonic ritual employed throughout the world. Some of them are called Emulation, Canadian Rite, York or American Rite. The latter is what most Grand Lodges in the United States endorse. But it doesn't matter what form of ritual is practiced. It's what is done with it that's important. The founders, whoever they were, of Speculative Masonry gave us a solid framework on which to build.

In the First Degree you were received with a warning. In the Second, with instructions in the manner in which you should deal with your fellowman. In the Third you are asked to reflect on man's moral and spiritual nature. And the Compasses take on a deeper meaning.

The Compasses begin at a point, draws a circle, and returns to the point where it began. It symbolizes the beginning, the span, and the end of life on earth. More important, it suggests the continuation of our existence. The immortality of the soul, an eternity with the Great Architect, becomes a reality.

The Compasses was a most important instrument to the operative master mason. By knowing how to use it fully made the difference between the master and a fellow of the craft. He used it to prove the squares of the workers. By drawing a circle with the compasses, taking

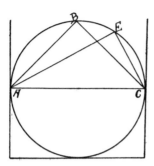

a straight edge and drawing a line through its center, then placing a dot (point) anywhere on the circle, a square can be checked for accuracy. The dot is connected with the line at both points where it crosses the circle. The result is a perfect right angle.

Our forefathers used the point within a circle to test the accuracy of their working tools. They erected cathedrals and public buildings that have stood the test of time. Speculative Masons use it to test their intentions and their conduct. We build Spiritual Buildings that hopefully will stand through eternity.

Your Circumambulation is longer. It gives you a greater opportunity to contemplate your Creator, to reflect on the days of your youth, and what you have accomplished in your manhood to this period. If you haven't been as productive as you should have been, you still have an opportunity to please your God before your spirit returns to Him.

Again, the Wardens and the Master give you an opportunity to decide whether or not you truly desire to devote your life to God, Freemasonry, your family, and your fellowman. This should give you cause to pause in later life when you find yourself straying from the obligations you assume. You weren't forced at any point to assume vows that would change your spiritual life. In fact, you stated that you knew what you entered Masonry to do. In brief, you promised to lead a better life than you ever had before.

You were caused to signify that you had learned the lessons of the Apprentice and Fellow of the Craft. Your days of probation are over. You are about to be entrusted with the knowledge of a Master Mason. Your squares are no longer oblong; they are perfect.

Symbolically, you spent seven years in learning that worldly attractions, money, and other material things are not important. They are only important if they can be used for the benefit of your fellowman. You went through a period of self-purification.

You then spent five more years, symbolically, in self-analysis. You learned to control your mind, your body, and your heart. You used the tools of architecture to square, level, and plumb your Spiritual Temple. You proved to your lodge that you were ready to search for Truth. You had squared your life and actions perfectly.

Your obligations now take on more and more responsibility. You find that as a Master Mason your charity, your love, must know no limits. Your family, friends, associates, widows, orphans, and especially your God, have a constant claim upon you. You can no longer think only of yourself. The circle drawn by the Compasses of Friendship, Morality, and Brotherly Love has no beginning. It has no ending.

You saw revealed once again the Three Great Lights in Masonry, the Volume of the Sacred Law, the Square and the Compasses. This time there was a difference. The Compasses were fixed so that they would ever remind you of your obligations. They were once again visible by aid of the Three Lesser Lights.

These Lesser Lights formed a triangle about the altar at which you knelt in reverence. They symbolized the presence of Deity. In all ages the triangle has been the symbol of God by whatever name He may have been called.

In those lodges where the Lesser Lights are placed about the altar, no one passes between the altar and the Worshipful Master. Symbolically, he receives his inspiration from the Great Lights and God. No obstruction should interfere with this inspiration.

The Masonic altar can be said to be one of sacrifice, as many altars were in religious ceremonies. You have taken obligations that have sacrificed your self-interest forevermore.

The Working Tools of a Master Mason, you learn, are "all the implements of Masonry indiscriminately." They are all that have been mentioned here, and many more. All have important symbolic lessons to impart to the Master Mason whose heart is receptive to the teachings of the Craft.

The Trowel does become the chief Working Tool of the Master Mason. He is taught to use it differently than his operative brethren. Instead of spreading cement, the Master Mason uses it symbolically to spread Brotherly Love and Affection. By doing this the Mystic Tie of Freemasonry becomes more binding. Its members are truly united into a Temple of Living Stones.

Brotherly Love is the first great tenet of Freemasonry. When this tenet captures the heart of a Master Mason he finds nothing effeminate in the love of one man for another. He finds beauty and inspiration in this love. It is encompassing and strong. It has stilled even battles so a brother, though an enemy in war, could be buried with Masonic rites.

Through Brotherly Love the Master Mason practices without the lodge those lessons taught within.

2

Emblems to Live By

Time, Patience, and Perseverance will accomplish all things, you are told. These are three of the virtues stressed in all training courses for leadership today. But scientific management was unknown when the ritual of Freemasonry was developed.

These virtues are emblematically represented by a monument of a beautiful virgin, weeping over a broken column. She holds a sprig of acacia in her right hand, an urn in her left. A book rests upon a broken column. A winged man, representing time, holds the virgin's hair. The ritual graphically explains the symbolism of this monument.

The ritual explanation of the urn held by the young lady is troublesome. It is especially so when you remember one of the points stressed in your obligation. According to Jewish law in the days of King Solomon, cremation wasn't tolerated. Bodies were buried outside the gates of the cities. *If* a monument was erected, and *if* there was an urn, it contained no ashes. It would have symbolized mourning, for small urns were used to catch the tears of those who mourned.

The idea of a monument to the memory of Hiram Abif may have been born about 1782. In 1817, John Barney (a Masonic lecturer born in Connecticut in 1780, active Masonically in Ohio) pictured a monument (without the broken column) similar to the one known today. Jeremy Ladd Cross (born in New Hampshire in 1783) added a broken column two years later. Both Barney and Cross were "disciples" of

THOMAS SMITH WEBB

1771–1819

Pioneer Ritualist and Lecturer for American Work

Thomas Smith Webb, who has been called the "father" of the ritual in America. Webb developed his version from the work of William Preston, an English ritualist, by abbreviating and revising Preston's lengthy lectures. Webb's work is followed today in most Grand Lodges.

Who developed the story attached to the Marble Monument, dedicated to the memory of Hiram Abif, appears to be unknown. It is generally credited to Webb. And if you will take into account that much of the ritual of Freemasonry is symbolic, the story can be accepted. It does symbolize Immortality. Many of the virtues of man are contained within the pages of books. In the case of the Monument, it would have been more accurate to have pictured a scroll, as books were unknown in the days of King Solomon.

You were told that our Institution is supported by three great pillars. They are called Wisdom, Strength, and Beauty. These "supports" are far older than the Masonic ritual. All three are indeed necessary if any organization is to prosper. So important did our Biblical Fathers consider the need for wisdom, it's mentioned 244 times in the Bible. And of all the wise men of ages past, none was considered wiser than King Solomon. It is natural, then, for the pillar in the East of a Masonic lodge to represent Solomon and symbolize Wisdom.

If there is any one thing that Freemasonry instills in its adherents above all else, it's the need for Wisdom. Few men achieve it, but all should strive for it. It can come only from knowledge, which comes from study, and experience. From the moment you entered a Masonic lodge as a candidate for the Entered Apprentice Degree, you have been studying, learning, and experiencing those things that help bring Wisdom. Your knowledge grows as you experience the lessons taught in the Master Mason Degree. By continued study of the ritual and all that lies behind it, your knowledge will increase.

The groundwork for your journey toward Wisdom has been laid. By continued study of Masonic philosophy, symbolism, and its history, you will be traveling toward the ultimate goal of Freemasonry—Wisdom in all things. Many men are knowledgeable, good and bad. Few men are wise. And no man who is really wise can be anything but good.

Without Strength, however, neither Wisdom nor Beauty can endure. This is not necessarily the strength that comes with brawn. It's a more subtle strength. It's passive. It's contained within the heart, mind, and soul of the man, himself. It's the strength of purpose, the ability to master one's self.

A weak foundation cannot support the framework and the pillars that hold a building together and give it support. The foundations and support for the Spiritual Building must be strong. This strength is composed, not of iron, steel, and timber, but of character. The operative mason chips away the unwanted material to fit it for the temporal building. The Speculative Mason uses the Common Gavel, and other implements of Masonry, symbolically, to form a Perfect Ashlar that will fit his Spiritual Building. He follows the Divine Plan in using the symbolic meaning of Masonry's second Great Pillar—Strength.

Beauty is symbolized in a Masonic lodge by the Corinthian column. It's the most beautiful of the ancient orders of architecture. But what beauty is has been debated since the beginning of time. What is attractive to you may be obnoxious to your neighbor. This is one reason why there are so many styles of automobiles and everything else that men can buy. Beauty is actually what the beholder believes it to be.

Again, it is necessary to look inwardly to determine the intent of Freemasonry. Again, it can't be material things, but spiritual beauty that the Master Mason should revere. Beauty of the mind, character, and spirit; beauty of the wonderful works of nature; glory of unselfishness, or idealism; the illumination of love.

You were told that the pillar of Wisdom was represented by the first Grand Master, Solomon, King of Israel. The Worshipful Master is the symbol of Wisdom in the lodge. Hiram, King of Tyre, symbolized

Strength because of the support he gave to King Solomon. The Senior Warden is this pillar of Strength in the lodge. Hiram Abif, because of his skillful work in brass and other metals, is classed as the third of the original Grand Masters and represented the pillar of Beauty. His counterpart in the lodge is the Junior Warden.

The legendary first three Grand Masters met periodically in the "Sanctum Sanctorum or Holy of Holies." The holiest place in Solomon's Temple was set aside for one article of furniture—the Ark of the Covenant. Within the Ark were kept the Ten Commandments upon two tablets of stone. The presence of God was believed to be more prevalent here than in any other place.

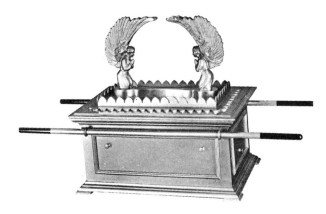

In a Masonic lodge the altar, with its Volume of the Sacred Law, Square and Compasses, symbolizes the Ark of the Covenant. The three Lesser Lights form a triangle symbolizing the presence of Deity.

There are three steps leading to the chair of the Worshipful Master in the East. You were told that these are emblematic of Youth, Manhood, and Old Age. These are symbolic of the three Degrees in Masonry, Entered Apprentice, Fellowcraft, and Master Mason. It is necessary to learn the lessons of these degrees well if you are to lead the life a good Master Mason should. You must learn, teach, and practice them if you are to one day climb these steps to preside in your lodge as its Worshipful Master.

You were told that the Pot of Incense is an emblem of a pure heart. Incense is, Masonically, symbolic of prayer, for you will read in Psalms 141:2, "Let my prayer be set forth before thee as incense; and the lifting up of my hands as the evening sacrifice." Of the five senses, part of the lessons of the Fellowcraft Degree, that of smell is most closely associated with emotions. Scents are reminders of pleasant experi-

ences, and some that aren't. The smell of flowers, wood smoke about the campfire, odors in the doctor's office or hospital, carry emotional memories for everyone.

The Pot which holds the incense is symbolic of Sacrifice. It means the giving up of selfishness and working for others. Purity of heart cannot be achieved without sincerity. Along with sincerity there must be love. Where there is love there must be high ideals. There must be a constant examination of one's self. No man should ever be content to stand still. He must never believe that he has reached the pinnacle of goodness, knowledge, or intelligence. He must never be satisfied with his accomplishments. He must continue to sacrifice his pleasures, his time, his material possessions for the betterment of his fellowman.

"Hands in Prayer"
By the famous 16th Century German Artist
Albrecht Durer. Original is in Vienna Museum

The Bee Hive, Masonically, is an emblem of Industry. The ritual recommends strongly that industry be practiced by all created beings. It tells us that we should never be content to be idle, especially when we can help our fellowman by exerting a little effort.

When and why the hive of the bee entered Freemasonry as a symbol no one knows. Much has been written on the subject. It has been pointed out that the hive pictured in all Masonic Monitors is man-made. The bee, however, does make the comb a geometrical perfection. Its six-sided cells provide more storage space for the honey from a weak material, wax, than could any other design. This is certainly a sign of industry and a symbol of Perfection.

In the book, *The Early Masonic Catechisms*, the bee in Masonry is mentioned as early as 1724 in an exposé printed in Ireland. It had this to say:

A *Bee* has in all Ages and Nations been the Grand *Hierogliphick* of *Masonry*, because it excells all other living Creatures in the Contrivance and Commodiousness of its *Habitation* or *Combe;* . . . nay *Masonry* or *Building* seems to be of the very Essence or Nature of the *Bee*, for her Building not the ordinary Way of all other living Creatures, is the Generative Cause which produces the Young ones (you know I suppose that *Bees* are of Neither Sex.)

For this Reason the Kings of *France* both *Pagans* and *Christians*, always Eminent *Free-Masons*, carried three *Bees* for their *Arms*. . . .

What *Modern Masons* call a *Lodge* was for the above Reasons by Antiquity call'd a HIVE of *Free-Masons*, and for the same Reasons when a Dissention happens in a *Lodge* the going off and forming another *Lodge* is to this Day call'd SWARMING. [The wording and spelling are the style as used in 1724.]

We must assume that the Bee Hive became an important symbol in Freemasonry the way the other symbols entered it. It symbolized what the cathedral builders did and the way they did it. The bee definitely is industrious. He works hard and tirelessly, not for himself, but for the swarm. He has a strength and knowledge of materials that cannot be duplicated. He works in complete cooperation, and without dissension, with his fellow bees. He protects the Queen, refuses admittance to enemies, builds, makes honey, and lives in a society ruled by law and order.

What bees do can be compared with the cathedral builders of centuries ago. The builders worked as a unit. No man worked for himself, but with his fellowmen to achieve a common goal. They worked under conditions that would stop modern architects and engineers. They had only man, beast, and ropes to put the pieces together. Every man had to do his part, his share, to take pride in his assignment, large or small. One man alone could accomplish little or nothing. Undoubtedly, the operative masons saw their duplicate in the bees. They could readily see in the honey-producers the symbol of the industry they, as builders of great cathedrals, practiced.

The Tiler's Sword is symbolic of a need in the days when this instrument was the principal means of offense or defense. It may have been used during the days of the operative masons to protect the secrets of the master builder from the cowan (an ignorant mason, one who laid stones without mortar, one who had not served the required time of apprenticeship; today an uninitiated man who poses as a Freemason). Now the Tiler simply refuses to admit a man into the lodge whom he doesn't know. The sword becomes a symbol of the Tiler's authority to protect the lodge from imposters.

To Speculative Masons, the Tiler's Sword should act as a reminder of moral lessons. It should admonish all of us to "set a guard at the entrance of our thoughts, to place a watch at the door of our lips, and to post a sentinel at the avenue of our actions, thereby excluding every unqualified and unworthy thought, word, and deed, and preserving consciences void of offense toward God and towards man."

The book of *Constitutions*, mentioned earlier, is not a symbol of secrecy. It contains the laws of Masonry. It's published for all to read. Every Master Mason should study the version approved by his Grand Lodge. It is considered so important that every Worshipful Master, upon his installation is charged to search this book at all times. He is also informed to "cause it to be read in your Lodge, that none may pretend ignorance of the excellent precepts it enjoins." If there is a symbol to be found in the book of *Constitutions*, it must be that of Masonic Law.

Silence and circumspection are considered Masonic virtues, according to the ritual. We are reminded to be ever "watchful and guarded in our words and actions." This is advice that should be followed under any circumstances. Not the enemies of Freemasonry, necessarily, are to be feared. The greater danger comes from the uninformed Mason. He has learned just enough to cause the Craft irreparable harm. Not always by saying too much, but often by saying too little. He knows so little about the Fraternity he believes everything is secret. Actually, there are few things that are secret.

Too often good men never petition a lodge because the member they asked about Freemasonry could, or would, tell them nothing. What the member should have done was to contact a well-informed brother, one who could discuss the teachings and principles of Masonry circumspectly and discreetly.

Remember the ritual instruction about the book of *Constitutions* guarded by the Tiler's Sword. But don't do it so zealously that you harm the Institution.

The All-Seeing Eye has been a symbol of Deity from the beginning of religion. The ancients adopted it from religion as a symbol of Deity for their "mysteries." From many ages has come the knowledge that the Great Architect of the Universe sees all, knows all, and controls all things. It is little wonder that the early ritualists associated this symbol with control of the sun, moon, stars, and comets. It reminds man that God is powerful, yet just, merciful, and loving.

When a Sword Pointing to a Naked Heart was added to the ritual is uncertain. It is referred to as a symbol of justice. It pointedly reminds us that God will reward us according to what we do in this life. But we know the rewards—the justice—will be tempered with mercy and understanding.

The Ark pictured in the ritual of Freemasonry is a representation of that of Noah. Masonically, it symbolizes the passing of the spirit of man from this life to one that is better and everlasting. Anciently, the symbolism was the same. Those who spent their lives in the service of their God, their country, and their fellowman could hope, and expect, to be safely wafted "over this tempestuous sea of troubles."

The Anchor is not only an ancient device, but also an ancient symbol. Masonically, it can be termed a symbol of safety. In the water, the anchor keeps a boat or ship from drifting by action of tide, wind, or current. Masonically, it can remind us to put our trust in Deity, to learn the lessons Masonry has to teach, and follow them faithfully. Then we shall be safely moored "in a peaceful harbor, where the wicked cease from troubling and where the weary shall find rest."

The Forty-seventh Problem of Euclid was brought into the ritual of Freemasonry for at least two reasons: 1. It was most important to the operative masons; 2. To extol some of the virtues of Pythagoras.

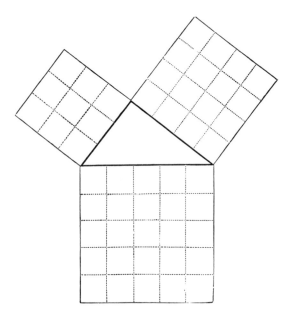

Euclid's 47th and 48th problems were necessary for the cathedral builders to understand because they read: "In every right angled triangle the square on the hypotenuse is equal to the sum of the squares on the other two sides. If the square described on one of the sides of a triangle is equal to the squares described on the other sides, then the angle contained by these two sides is a right angle."

This is the root of all geometry, the foundation of mathematics. It has made it possible for railroads, tunnels, roads, bridges to be built from both sides and join perfectly in the middle. The astronomer, navigator, engineer, mathematician would be lost without the 47th Problem to point the way. Is it any wonder Pythagoras shouted "Eureka"?

Who was this man Pythagoras whom operative and Speculative Masons revered? You were told that he was a traveler, a philosopher, and a mathematician seeking knowledge. But he was much more. He was an astronomer, a teacher and the founder of a school, a man who many writers claim performed miracles. He believed in the immortality of the soul. He was an outstanding athlete. He became so wise and learned that his teachings were followed by such giants of the ancient world as Socrates, Plato, and Aristotle. He did more for his century than any other man.

Like many great men, Pythagoras left no writings of his own. What he did, and what is known about him, has been handed down through the writings of his followers. There were many of them. There still are. To some extent, Masonic lodges of today are patterned after the society he formed. The philosophy he taught in the Fifth Century B.C. is much the same as the philosophy taught Freemasons in this Twentieth Century A.D.

Pythagoras is credited with many accomplishments other than the discovery of the 47th Problem of Euclid. Weights and measures were introduced into Greece by Pythagoras. The doctrine now known as the "harmony of the spheres" originated with him. He discovered the therapeutical value of music. He was the first to carry the study of arithmetic beyond the needs of commerce. The term "philosopher" was first used by him. There is evidence that no one considered the earth a sphere revolving in space before him. He founded the "Pythagorean Fraternity," the most influential school of its time. He was the first to consider women the equal of men, and admitted both to his school on equal terms. He was probably the first to teach by parables and symbols.

Archytas, a Greek philosopher of about 400 B.C., said that Pythagoras spoke to a group of politicians in these words:

The best laws and constitutions must be a composite of all constitutions, and contain something democratic, oligarchic, monarchic, and aristocratic. . . . The true chief must not only possess the science and power of commanding well, but he must also love men; for it is absurd that a shepherd should hate his flock, and feel hostile disposition towards those he is educating.

We must first know that the good man is not thereby necessarily happy, but that the happy man is necessarily good; for the happy man is he who deserves praise and congratulations; the good man deserves only praise.

Pythagoras might well have been speaking to all Freemasons, particularly those who are the leaders of the Craft.

What does the 47th Problem of Euclid symbolize? Perseverance; a search for Truth; the need for more and more knowledge. By understanding the full meaning behind this symbol, we can determine the reason the Square is the emblem worn by the leader of the lodge—the Worshipful Master. We also know why the Square is mentioned as a symbol of many things throughout the ritual.

The Hour Glass, as explained in the ritual, is a gloomy subject. But when you look at it as a part of the whole philosophy of Freemasonry, it isn't dreary. It becomes a symbol of Time—time profitably spent.

Time is the only thing that men have in equal abundance. As you learned in the First Degree, time is important. Each day should be divided into portions. It should be used toward the service of God and your fellowman. It should be used wisely, for every second wasted is lost forever. Time is one commodity that can never be recovered.

The Scythe, too, is ritualistically a gloomy instrument, and you were told it is an emblem of time. It is interesting to note that the Hour Glass and Scythe were not symbols employed by operative masons. They are, in fact, of comparatively recent origin. They won't be found in any but the rituals of this country. Thomas Smith Webb had his reasons for adding them, but outside of his explanation in the ritual no one knows why. It speaks of "havoc," "cuts the brittle thread of life," and "devouring scythe of time."

But even with those foreboding words, hope is held out for mankind. By using time during our youth and manhood wisely to acquire knowledge, by putting this knowledge to use for God and man during our years of manhood, our rewards will be great. We will achieve immortality. We will be "gathered into the land where our fathers have gone before us."

The Scythe, too, is a symbol of Time. It is also a symbol of Learning, and of Immortality.

In many rituals a Spade, Setting Maul, Coffin, and Sprig of Acacia are explained together. The first three are obviously symbols of Death or Mortality. Just as obviously this is something that must come to all of God's creatures. But Freemasonry, through its teachings and philosophy, holds out hope for everyone. It believes in Immortality, as symbolized by the Sprig of Acacia.

The grave is the end of life on this planet, but it's not the end of man. The body will decay and disintegrate. Man will return to dust. But something within man, soul, spirit, or call it what you will, never, never dies. That part of man that has absorbed the teachings of Freemasonry, and put them into daily practice, will live forever.

The Sprig of Acacia symbolizes Faith—faith in the immortality of man, faith in the promises made by God in His Volume of the Sacred Law.

3

Freemasonry's Great Legend

You actively participated in one of the greatest dramas of all time. Many, many of the most renowned men who preceded you as the central character in this drama that no man can ever forget have made this claim. One of them, Edwin T. Booth, the famous Shakespearean actor, made this statement:

"In all my research and study, in all my close analysis of the masterpieces of Shakespeare, in my earnest determination to make those plays appear real on the mimic stage, I have never, and nowhere, met tragedy so real, so sublime, so magnificent as the legend of Hiram. It is substance without shadow—the manifest destiny of life which requires no picture and scarcely a word to make a lasting impression upon all who can understand. To be Worshipful Master, and to throw my whole soul into that work, with the candidate for my audience and the Lodge for my stage, would be a greater personal distinction than to receive the plaudits of the people in the theatres of the world."

The lessons found in the Legend of Hiram Abif reach to the roots of the soul and spirit. They are instilled in the heart forever. You were an active participant, so that these lessons would be deeply implanted, never to be lost.

You represented an historical Biblical character. What transpires is, however, a legend, a drama, an allegory. It depicts man's search for truth, for courage, for prudence, for his immortal soul.

There are other characters in this drama. And you find that they are much the same as men today. Some are leaders, trying to impress the teachings of Deity upon the hearts of those who are subordinate to them. Others have learned these lessons well and endeavor to pass them along to those with whom they come in contact. A few are evil. They see no good in anything. They connive to reap the rewards of those who carry out their obligations, without fulfilling their own.

The ultimate triumph of good over evil, and life over death, has been depicted throughout the ages in drama, song, and story. Legends depicting a central figure being killed and then returned to life were common to many religions and rites. These undoubtedly had a bearing on the development of the lessons the ritualists of Freemasonry believed had to be taught. But the Hiramic Legend is more intense, moralistic, and meaningful than any that preceded it.

Nothing existing today is unconnected with the past. The connection may be remote, but it's still there. The philosophy of Freemasonry is closely connected with the past. It has preserved, fortunately, the wisdom it took centuries for man to acquire. Masonry, through its symbolism, has kept this wisdom alive. It allows men to interpret this symbolism as his mind and heart dictate. It leaves men free to speculate, to think, to create.

Hiram Abif did exist. He was a skillful worker in brass and other metals. He was sent to assist King Solomon by Hiram, King of Tyre. The Bible tells us this. So does Flavius Josephus. Many of the old *Gothic Constitutions* (documents about Masonry written from 1390 A.D. to the 18th Century) mention Hiram Abif in some form.

The Hiram Abif who actually worked at beautifying the Temple of Solomon lived to old age! He died of natural causes!

The Masonic Hiram Abif was "born"—and died—to instill in the hearts, minds, and souls of Freemasons symbolic lessons of life. These include, but aren't limited to, Perseverance, Love of mankind, Courage, Patience, Devotion to God, Fortitude, Justice, Fidelity to a trust, and the Immortality of Man. He is symbolic of what happens to man day by day.

The great work in the Temple that Hiram was engaged in is symbolic of the work you, and all men, do daily. As he supervised the workmen, so you supervise and organize your life, dreams, and hopes. The enemies he encountered—greed, jealousy, and selfishness—you meet constantly. As he wasn't always victorious, neither will you be. But the hope that was held out for him will be held out for you, if you, like him, are faithful to your trust.

You noted, as you participated in the drama, many things that no one else can explain to you. You are an individual, as are all men. What one sees and feels another won't. This is one of the many beauties of the philosophy called "Freemasonry." Its symbols have a variety of meanings for everyone. What is taught becomes suggestions to be explored further as you grow in wisdom.

It is interesting to note that Hiram's enemies came from the inner circle—the workers whom he trusted. So do most of any man's adversaries. He will usually guard himself against attacks from those he believes he must fear, but has no reason to protect himself from those he loves and trusts.

Hiram's friends and brothers, also from the inner circle, endeavored to come to his rescue. He had been a man who lived for others. He

"The Murder of Hiram"
From the original painting by A. J. Knapp. Courtesy
of Philosophical Research Society Library, Los Angeles

gave of himself, his time, his talent, and his love. The fact that he created beauty speaks for itself in determining the type of man he was. Such devotion could not go unrewarded. And his greatest reward was in the friends he created in high and low places.

As Hiram prayed daily for guidance from his God before drawing the designs that would set the craftsmen to work, so must we. When we pray, we recognize a Superior Being, one who can help us to achieve all things. Through the Great Architect of the Universe, we can acquire the self-image we must have if we are to be successful. Through prayer, we learn to meditate, to take stock of our strengths and weaknesses. By concentrating on our strengths, we can accomplish great things for our fellowman.

Until a man learns to pray for himself, he cannot hope to learn the supreme Masonic secret. It is through prayer, and through living what Freemasonry teaches, that this secret will come to life. Through these teachings the Mason will put into practice the Brotherhood of Man under the Fatherhood of God. In doing so, he will develop his character and personality in the image of the Great Architect of the Universe.

This is perhaps the greatest lesson taught through the Hiramic Legend.

Hiram drew his designs for the building and beautifying of the Temple in the Sanctum Sanctorum, or Holy of Holies. There he received the inspiration he needed because he felt the presence of God. There he could concentrate without being disturbed.

Man, in order to build and improve his Spiritual Temple, must do so in the presence of God. He, too, must find a retreat where he can concentrate and meditate. In his retreat, man can let God help him draw the designs that will improve his life. There he can ponder the lessons and "secrets" he has learned from the ritual of the Craft.

What are these lessons and secrets of Freemasonry? Each will see something a little differently. This is as it should be. But all will see that the great secret of Freemasonry is found in its first Tenet, Brotherly Love. This Tenet encompasses the Wisdom, Strength, and Beauty which are the pillars that hold the fabric of Speculative Masonry together.

Each Master Mason becomes his own architect. Each supervises the building of that "temple not made by hands." Each builds into his structure beauty, harmony, and knowledge to the extent he is willing to work.

Through the "secrets" of the Fraternity, we learn that nothing constructive can ever be gained by force. Violence destroys; it never builds. It's much easier to be a wrecker than a builder. The poet, G. K. Chesterton, showed this when he had a building-wrecking foreman say: "They can easily wreck in a day or two / What builders have taken years to do!"

Man will always encounter wreckers, ruffians, enemies anxious to extort from him his good name, or to acquire something without working for it. There will always be those who will try, through force or otherwise, to make others compromise their fidelity to their trust. When this force comes from those who are loved and trusted, the evil is greater. There is little defense that can be offered, because no need for a defense was anticipated.

Too often the enemy will endeavor to destroy freedom of speech, and that can prove a mortal blow. When a man's throat is silenced, it is difficult to carry on his activities efficiently. Others will try to maim a person with blows to the heart. The heart is not only a vital organ, but symbolically holds all that is good, or divine, in man. By dulling or killing this divine light, man becomes useless.

A blow to the head, or brain, is the worst that man can suffer. It destroys freedom of thought. This creates ignorance. There is no greater enemy than ignorance. Where there is ignorance, there is despotism. A few control the many. These few use the majority as pawns in their quest for power, and more power.

There is something of a ruffian in all men. The good and the bad are constantly at war with each other in hearts and minds. Physical blows aren't always necessary to destroy another. Half-truths, outright lies, and vicious gossip can break a victim's heart or destroy his good name. The symbolism of the Tiler's Sword should be ever foremost in the mind of the Master Mason.

The Legend of Hiram Abif teaches all Freemasons that to betray a trust is a fate worse than death itself. It reminds man that he should live each day prepared to die, and die as a man prepared to live forever.

The lessons of the necessity of leadership are plainly visible throughout the Ritual of Masonry. Again, we find that Freemasonry was far ahead of its time. It taught "scientific management" centuries ago. The outside world didn't discover the need for utilizing management until the early 1900's. Since then thousands of books have been written on the subject.

Without leadership, someone to lay out plans and set the workers on the proper course, there is confusion and chaos. When the leader is absent, work comes to a standstill until someone else takes over. It is little wonder that King Solomon was greatly disturbed when his superintendent was nowhere to be found. It appeared that all was lost. Plans had to be abandoned. Building activities had ceased. Craftsmen were idled.

This is symbolic of human beings. When an active part of the body is stilled because of injury, sickness, disease, or sorrow, some functions stop. Hatred, resentment, jealousy, and prejudice keep the brain (each man's leader) from drawing meaningful designs on the Spiritual Trestleboard. They create confusion among the organs of the body. Chaos results. Creativity is impossible.

Fortunately, there is a symbolic Sprig of Acacia to be found. When one finds this symbol of Immortality he can exclaim, as did Pythagoras, "Eureka!" He has found success. He has achieved his goal. One of his searches is over. He has triumphed over the enemies within his mind and soul. He is well on the way to determining what that elusive word "Truth" is.

There is no quick and easy path to follow in the search for the branch of acacia. Each man must set his own goals and draw his own designs to achieve those goals. It's comforting to know, however, that he can call on his brethren for assistance and advice. They can give him a sense of direction. They can give him moral support and enthusiastic backing. They can give him ideas with which to work. But no one can make another's decisions for him. The final course is one he must set himself.

It is comforting to know that Freemasonry lets no man travel alone. There is always a trusted friend and Brother to help guide him along a safe path. This has been pointed out in each of the three degrees. Brotherly Love will always win over adversity.

The search for that which is lost will go on forever. There are always new "worlds" to be conquered. Changes are taking place every second. Most of these changes affect each person in some way. Freemasonry's great quest for Truth will always be elusive. For when Truth is found in one area, another area will be opened for exploration. This is what Freemasonry teaches. It is one of the most important lessons to be found in the Master Mason Degree. The Master Mason must continuously search for the unknown. He, and the Fraternity, will then progress. When he stands still, he will stagnate; so will the Craft.

In the Third Degree drama, the men who overruled the moral lessons they had been taught by letting their passions get out of control, were brought to justice. They received the punishment they suggested. The lesson for all is plain. Each man has good and evil within him. He must always be conscious of this. He must keep his moral attributes

"Attempting an Escape"   *"Brought to Justice"*

in command. If he doesn't, he is turning his "enemies" loose. They will eventually destroy him spiritually, morally, or physically.

The search of the Fellowcrafts ended in what appeared to be a tragedy. A good man had fallen a victim of his foes. But the will to win which is buried deeply within every man proved victorious. Through prayer, the will of God, and with the assistance of friends even the grim tyrant, Death, was defeated.

God said, through Job, in the ritual: "For there is hope of a tree, if it be cut down, that it will sprout again, and that the tender branch thereof will not cease." Isn't it logical to believe that God will do as much for man as he will for a tree?

Freemasonry teaches the immortality of man; the resurrection of the body and eternal life, if a man have faith in the *merits* of the Lion of

the Tribe of Judah. It is claimed that Solomon was once symbolic of the Lion of the Tribe of Judah. An emulation of his merits, philosophy, love of God, and wisdom will assure his followers of an exemplary life in this world. While living as Solomon did, any man will be able to "Welcome the grim tyrant Death, and receive him as a kind messenger sent from our Supreme Grand Master, to translate us from this imperfect, to that all perfect, glorious, and celestial Lodge above."

The Five Points of Fellowship are important to follow if you are to be a dedicated Master Mason, a "living stone" in the Temple of Freemasonry. By following them you will be emulating the symbolic first Grand Master.

A brother will readily go out of his way, on foot if necessary, to assist a distressed Master Mason, or any person who needs his help. How far should you go? The limitation must be placed by you. No one else can answer the question for you. It's your conception of Brotherly Love that counts.

Freemasonry has taught you to pray for yourself, something you probably knew how to do in your youth. Freemasonry also teaches you to pray for your brother and others. Remembering your brother's welfare as well as your own can have far-reaching effects. A few years ago a group of Masonic leaders, mostly Grand Masters, were meeting in a convention. Word reached them that the wife of one of their members had been seriously, almost surely mortally, stricken. After several minutes of stunned silence, one took the hand of the man whose wife was dying and said, "Let's pray." The others linked hands with them. Each offered his petition to God for the recovery of the wife. Miraculously, the crisis passed while these men prayed! She was restored to live a full and happy life.

The psychoanalyst's reclining chair has claimed far too many men and women, simply because they had no one else to confide in. Bottling up problems is something few people can live with. It's the worst kind of loneliness. It produces negative thoughts and feelings. It breeds an unhealthy self-image. It eats away the soul and mind. Freemasonry recognized this centuries before there were doctors who specialized in abnormal mental reactions due to repression. You are, therefore, charged to keep a brother's secrets when confided to you as such. Just your sympathetic silence can help him through a crisis.

Regrettably, the word "secret" has an evil connotation in the minds of too many people. The "secret" may be simply an ambition, an idea, a hope, a desire. But even if the secret is one of guilt, the brother's trust in you must not be violated. To betray the confidence placed in you would be unforgivable. To keep his secret may cost you sleepless

"Man Helping Man"

This bronze plaque, wrought in the foundry of Maurice J. Power, New York, is the tablet on the 66th New York Regiment marker on the battlefield at Gettysburg, Pa.

It represents a Federal soldier holding his canteen to the lips of a wounded Confederate soldier with his left hand, while with his right he grasps the hand of his former enemy. In a scroll above the scene are the words: PEACE & UNITY. A close examination will disclose much more.

nights, but it must be kept. The only one who can release you from this trust is the brother, himself.

In actuality, you have also told your brethren that they can count on you to stretch forth your hand to keep them from falling. You have offered them your strength, your ability, your knowledge when they need it. There are no reservations. It matters not whether the aid they need is mental, physical, or monetary. Your promise contains no "buts."

When a brother is in danger of any kind, it is your duty to advise him of his impending peril. In doing so, you must remember that it is not by *your* "plumb line" that you judge him, but by *his.* And it is *his* Square and *his* Level, not yours, by which you are to determine his actions. His opinions may differ from yours politically or religiously, but they are his tools, not yours. When he goes astray from *his principles,* then and only then, should you quietly remind him that he is in error. Then you should assist him to find the right track for *him* to follow.

The concepts of Brotherly Love are to be found in the Five Points of Fellowship. By following them you will help, aid, and assist every brother who might need your support. You will defend your brother against attacks by others, verbal or physical. You will guard his good name as your own. You will do these things and more—much more.

By doing so you will be following the symbolic teachings of the Working Tools of a Master Mason. You have been taught that they are all the implements used by operative masons and Speculative Masons. The Trowel is set apart, however. The ritual tells you it is to be used, symbolically, to spread "the cement of Brotherly Love and Affection, which unites us into one sacred band or society of friends and Brothers—a Temple of living stones, among whom no contention should ever exist."

It is important to remember that it is Brotherly Love, the principal ingredient in Freemasonry, that unites men of every country, sect, and opinion into a great Fraternity. It is Brotherly Love, in every sense that phrase implies, that can unite the world into one circle with a common interest—peace on earth and goodwill to all men.

These are some of the important lessons to be found in the symbolism of the three degrees in Freemasonry. Learn them well. Teach them to all men everywhere.

—So Mote It Be—